P9-CDD-198

SEX-ROLE PSYCHOLOGY

Psychology Series

Clinical Child Psychology
   Williams, J., Ph.D. and Gordon, S., Ph.D. (Eds.)

Directory of Unpublished Experimental Mental Measures, Vol. 1
   Goldman, B. A., Ed.D. and Saunders, J. L. (Eds.)

Dynamic Personal Adjustment: An Introduction
   Sachs, H.L., Ph.D.

Environmental Psychology and Nonverbal Behavior
   Lee, R.M., Ph.D. (Ed.)

In Quest of a New Psychology
   Johnson, R.E., Ph.D.

Journal of School Psychology
   Phillips, B.N., Ph.D.

Language in Behavior
   Howell, R.W., Ph.D., and Vetter, H.J., Ph.D.

Pastoral Psychology
   Mills, L.O. Th.D.

Psychology of Women Quarterly
   Babladelis, G., Ph.D. (Ed.)

Sex-Role Psychology
   Wesley, F., Ph.D. and Wesley, C.

SEX-ROLE PSYCHOLOGY

Frank Wesley
Claire Wesley

HUMAN SCIENCES PRESS
Formerly BEHAVIORAL PUBLICATIONS INC.
72 FIFTH AVENUE, NEW YORK, N.Y. 10011

BF
692.2
.W47

Library of Congress Catalog Number 77-1308

ISBN: 0-87705-307-3

Copyright © 1977 by Human Sciences Press
72 Fifth Avenue, New York, New York 10011

Printed in the United States of America
789   987654321
Library of Congress Cataloging in Publication Data

Library of Congress Cataloging in Publication Data

Wesley, Frank, 1918–
    Sex-role psychology.

    Includes bibliographical references.
    1. Sex role. I. Wesley, Claire, joint author.
II. Title. [DNLM: 1. Identification (Psychology)
BF692 W513]
BF692.2.W47   155.3'3   77-1308
ISBN 0-87705-307-3

94948

ACKNOWLEDGMENT

We would like to acknowledge the support we have received from colleagues and friends at Portland State University and at the University of Hamburg, Germany. We are especially grateful to Mary Rose for the inspiration she has given us to explore the subject of sex-roles and to Melvin McCann for encouraging us to write this text. We are indebted to Ann-Katrein Miessner, Eckart Mildenstein, Rose Pointon, and John Stopford for reviewing and editing the manuscript and for giving us much helpful advice.

F. W.
C. W.

To Irene Wolfson
successful as an economist and teacher
understanding as our mother and grandmother

CONTENTS

Chapter 1

EQUALIZATION AND PSYCHOLOGY

In 1977 there was not a single woman among the 100 members of the U.S. Senate, only two among the 50 state governors, and none among the nine U.S. Supreme Court justices. At the same time males were arrested ten times more frequently than women, were committed to prison twenty times as frequently, and made up 85 per cent of the defendants in juvenile courts. The discrepancies in other countries are just as striking as those in the United States. In England, for instance, only 44 of the 3,281 highest-ranking professors are women. In Switzerland, skilled female laborers receive only 60 per cent of the salary their male colleagues receive. In West Germany almost twice as many men as women obtain the high school diploma required for study at a university and there are about 36,000 male prisoners as compared to only 1,000 female prisoners in West German penal institutions (Blackstone & Fuller, 1975; Held & Levy, 1974; Statistisches Jahrbuch, 1975). Such striking examples show beyond doubt that gross differences exist between females and males, and they suggest that there is a psychological difference between men and women. It is the purpose of this book to examine the origins and the modes of these differences in the hope that such a study will contribute to the cultural and economic equality of the sexes.

The Psychology of Women

Psychology is the study of the human mind, and when it was formally established as an academic discipline in Leipzig in 1875 it aimed to investigate the mind's consciousness by examining the attributes of sensation, neural reactions, visual and auditory perception, and the nature of learning. At that time sex differences in these particular subject matters were neither postulated nor found, and it is understandable that there was no interest in a separate psychology of women nor in the study of sex-role differences.

It was not until after the turn of the century—and influenced by American pragmatism—that the emphasis in psychology began to shift from the investigation of the structure and attributes of the mind toward the function of human individuals in society. It may be argued in retrospect that a separate psychology of women might have been useful at that time because females and males had many different social attitudes and functions. We can only speculate why the psychology of women did not arise as a separate area of study and why there was no interest in a sex-role psychology. After the turn of the century psychologists were "modern," scientific people wanting to disprove some of the commonly held stereotypes about women being more mythical, intuitive, and emotional. Hence differences were deemphasized, and many studies were aimed at pointing out the existing similarities.

It is not clear whether it was the depression that

preceded World War II, the economic boom that followed it, or other social conditions that obviated the woman's role in the work force and crystallized her role more and more as wife and mother and the male's role as supporter working in nondomestic areas. In spite of these distinct social functions a psychology of women still did not appear as a separate study area. Perhaps there was little incentive as the sexes appeared more or less satisfied in their respective roles. Females were studied in connection with attitudes toward marriage and motherhood and males were examined in relation to work interests, aptitudes, and motivation. When studies did find sex differences they reported them generally as isolated facts without speculating about their origin or concern about their consequences. As will be discussed later in more detail (see Chapter 8), psychologists generally "played along" with the existing social currents assuming that an individual's normality is indicated by the degree he or she conforms to the established cultural sex-role norms—whatever they were.

The interest in a separate study of the psychology of women arose with the event of the women's liberation movement in the 1960s making many women aware that the roles in which society had cast them were in many ways disadvantageous to them. In order to obtain equality many women felt they had to compete against men or at least alter their own existing attitudes and behavior. This desire to be equal may well be responsible for the quest for a psychology of women. A knowledge of the differences as well as the similarities between the sexes seems essential for the move towards equality. Thus the study of women and sex-roles includes data and observation on males. For example, we could not know that women live almost eight years longer than men had we not the life expectancy data for both, which at birth are about 68 years for males and

76 years for females. Many other behavioral and attitudinal data will have to be collected on both males and females in order to suggest ways to overcome certain sex-role stereotypes held in common by both males and females.

Although there was no separate study area concerning the psychology of women for almost 100 years, there have always been women participating in the study of psychology. Anna Berliner (b. 1888) received her doctorate in 1913 at the University of Leipzig in Germany. She contributed a lifetime of research and teaching in the areas of perception and ophthalmology. There was also Bluma Zeigarnik (b. 1900) who studied in Germany and who has held the directorship of the Institute of Psychiatry at the University of Moscow for several decades. In 1894, in America, Margaret Floy Washburn (1871–1939) received the first Ph.D. degree ever awarded in psychology at Cornell University. Her work pioneered experimental and animal psychology. Mary Whiton Calkins (1863–1930) authored five major texts and wrote several important critiques on Gestalt Psychology (Calkins, 1926). Christine Ladd-Franklin (1847–1930) became well known for her contribution to the theory of color vision (Ladd-Franklin, 1929). All three women—Ladd-Franklin, Calkins, and Washburn—were mentioned as top-ranking psychologists in the "American *Men* of Science" (authors' italics) covering the period from 1903 to 1940. Other women like Mary Cover Jones (b. 1898) and Elizabeth Hurlock (b. 1898) began working in the area of experimental child psychology in the 1920s. Hurlock's text on *Child Development* was first published in 1942 and had reached its fifth edition by the 1970s. Karen Horney (1885–1953) became a famous psychoanalyst challenging some of Freud's biological assumption in favor of social influences. Many more influential women psychologists will be mentioned throughout this text. Although the number of women psychologists has been small compared to their male counterparts, there are presently more women in psychology (27 per cent) than in any other academic profession.

Sex–Roles

There are some obvious and some not so obvious biological differences between females and males, but the psychological differences center mainly around the culturally established sex-roles. The psychology of women depends a great deal on the study of sex-roles, on knowing how they are established, how they influence the sexes to think, feel, and act differently, and how they can best be altered.

The study of sex-role psychology has been closely linked to the interest in the psychology of women. Since the early 1970s about one quarter of all U.S. colleges and universities offer courses in "Sex-Role Psychology" and another quarter give instructions in the "Psychology of Women." In many instances the course content of these two courses is similar, containing such topics as sex-role development, sex-role stereotypes and behaviors, and sex-roles related to performance, personality, and conflicts.

The number of sex-role studies has increased tenfold in the past decade from about 50 reported in the *Psychological Abstracts* in 1965 to about 500 reported in 1975; the journal of *Sex Roles,* under the editorship of Phyllis Katz, devoted to articles relating to the sociology and psychology of sex-roles, was founded in 1975. The studies on sex-role differences extend into such diverse psychological areas as developmental, educational, adolescent, and vocational psychology. The methods of investigation used in these areas are just as varied. They include historical and theoretical approaches, comparative and physiological data, free observation, questionnaires, and results of interviews.

Arline Hochschild has reviewed (1973) the research on sex-roles and believes it can be categorized into the following four main perspectives: (1) Sex differences investigated by psychologists such as emotion, cognition, and traits; (2) Sex-role norms that govern role strain, role models, and role conflicts; (3) Women as a minority group; and (4) The "politics of cast," which investigates power differences. Hochschild's categorization based on sociological views is somewhat arbitrary. She herself points out that investigators with various perspectives in mind may examine the same sex-role phenomenon using entirely different vocabularies. What is called a "feminine trait" by one investigator is called a "role element" or a "minority characteristic" by others.

The treatment of sex-role studies in the present text shall avoid the above-mentioned classifications. Studies will be enumerated in a developmental order. Those pertaining to infancy and childhood will be mentioned first followed by those concerning schools and vocations. We shall also attempt to avoid the use of different vocabularies by minimizing the citation of nonobjective studies and the usage of abstract and generalized terms. Whenever possible a sex-role trait or stereotype will be identified by the way it was measured or observed, by the questions asked to identify it, and by the group examined.

As in other psychological research the knowledge about the origin of sex-roles is greatly hampered by the fact that humans cannot be raised in an isolated environment or in environments that are 100 per cent equal. As compared to animals humans have a long developmental period needing a year before they can walk and about two years before they can talk. It is difficult for psychologists to find out what impression the environment makes on the child during this relatively long maturational period. After the child is able to walk and talk, environmental variation increases due to individual interactions with relatives, peers, teachers, and television, and it becomes even more difficult for psychologists to single out simple cause-and-effect relationships.

Research Methods

In order to obtain knowledge on causality psychologists use such various experimental techniques as cross-sectional, longitudinal, cross-cultural, and cross-species methods, which often allow them to assess cause-and-effect relationships in indirect ways. The *cross-sectional* method frequently used in the investigation of sex-roles examines different age groups at the same time. Rather than waiting years to find out how, for instance, a group of infants will behave in their later childhood, a group of infants and a group of school-age children are examined and compared at the same time. This type of study will often narrow the search for causal factors although it is susceptible to errors due to the changes in cultural trends. For example, it has been shown that at birth girls move their mouths more often than boys, that they babble and vocalize more in early infancy (Moss, 1967), that they surpass boys in verbal subjects during school years, and that they make slightly better scores on verbal IQ items during adulthood (Maccoby & Jacklin, 1974). If the results of a number of experiments conducted with groups differing in age fall into a certain pattern, the researcher may venture guesses about certain connections. With the cross-sectional data given above a pscyhologist may want to suggest that females have a tendency to be more verbal.

Another technique is the *longitudinal* approach where one and the same group of individuals is observed over a period of years and where records are kept on certain of their own and their environments' characteristics. One such study, the Berkeley Growth Study, has been in progress for 40 years and has yielded among other findings some interesting sex-role data. As reported by Nancy Bayley (1968) girls seem to develop somewhat more steadily and more predictably than boys and seem to be less influenced by their family environment.

Another frequently used technique to discover causal relationships in the formation of sex roles is the *cross-cultural* method. When variables cannot be controlled within one culture, experimenters seek other cultures or subcultures to factor out certain conditions. Madigan (1957), for example, who was interested in investigating the causes of the differential life span of men and women, conducted such a cross-cultural research study. It is a statistical fact that women in our society live 7.7 years longer than men. Since men suffer more frequent heart attacks than women, it was often assumed that they die sooner because they experience more emotional stresses in their struggle to earn a living. To test this hypothesis Madigan investigated the life-span differences by comparing the vital statistics of 9,000 cloistered inhabitants. He reasoned that environmental conditions are much more equal for both nuns and monks in this subculture than for men and women in the general society. A shorter average life span of monks, for instance, could not be attributed to the emotional stress associated with an aggressive business world or with family responsibilities. Since Madigan found that monks die seven years earlier than nuns, he concluded that the sex differences in longevity are mainly biological and not caused by the environment.

It is interesting to make cross-cultural comparisons about vocational customs. In the Soviet Union, for instance, more than 80 per cent of all medical doctors are women as compared to 9 per cent in the United States. There are also great national differences in the relative number of female dentists, with 1 per cent in the United States, 20 per cent in most Nordic countries, and 87 per cent in the Soviet Union (Judith Blake, 1974). Such cross-cultural comparisons show clearly that the medical and dental professions can be successfully practiced by women and that it is not a lack of innate capacities or skills that causes women in the United States to be in such a minority as dentists and doctors.

We could also learn from other cultures methods by which certain professional equalities can be obtained, especially if we further compare educational and motivational factors. Dodge in his book *Women in the Soviet Economy* (1966) lists the shorter hours (the medical profession works in four six-hour shifts) and a more flexible work schedule as some of the incentives for Russian women to select a medical or dental career. Female physicians in the Soviet Union do not seem to have the subordinate role an assumption often made by Americans. Dodge reports that 57 per cent of all chief physicians of medical establishments in the Soviet Union are women.

A comparison of the educational systems may give further clues as to the reasons for the prevalence of female dentists and physicians in the Soviet Union and to the scarcity of their counterparts in the United States. In Soviet high schools, science subjects are not electives; every graduate—male and female—has had at least four full years of physics, chemistry, biology, and mathematics. This gives all high school graduates the prerequisites for studying medicine, dentistry, or any other science. If they choose not to pursue those subjects it is not because they lack the skills to begin them. In the United States, the freedom of choosing school subjects may play peculiar tricks: Although the Soviet student has fewer choices during the high-school years, he or she has more choices after graduation.

Much knowledge about human psychology has been obtained by comparing different species of animals. This *cross-species* method is frequently used in the study of sex-roles with the aim of revealing our "real" nature—how we would feel and behave had we not been influenced by cultural mores and ideologies. Cross-species comparisons have always aroused great popular and scientific interests from Aesop's animal fables to the Darwinian theory of evolution. Scientifically, however, such comparisons are a delicate matter, especially when we try to compare psychological traits.

In many aspects animals and humans are alike, physiologically as well as psychologically. In medicine, before the event of synthetic insulin, for example, diabetics depended entirely on the insulin obtained from the cow's pancreas. In psychology it has been found that animals and humans are much alike when we compare the ways they learn. On learning a maze, for instance, rats will first master the alleyways at the beginning and at the end. Similarly, humans learning a poem will also master first the beginning and the ending verses. In conditioning, both animals and humans will learn to respond to a new signal fastest if it is presented half a second before the reward (or punishment).

Many more examples of similarities could be cited, but there are also many dissimilarities. Comparisons with chimpanzees indicate that the main difference lies in the human capacity to form linguistic concepts by which we can guide our behavior and which we can use to reinforce our thoughts and actions in rational (and also in irrational) ways. We can derive gratification and anxieties from our own thought processes and fantasies that can often be quite independent from our momentary environment. Humans as compared to subhumans depend to a much greater degree on learned habits than on physiological drives as we can measure them. For example, it has been attempted (Glass & Johnson, 1944) to change the homosexual behavior of males by injecting them with male sex hormones. It was reasoned that homosexual males prefer males because they are like females lacking androgens, the male sex hormones. Booster doses of androgens given to homosexuals did increase their sexual drive but also their continued contact with homosexuals. Thus, the hormone influenced the underlying drive, but it did not change the learned habit by which this drive had been satisfied in the past.

If we humans study animals to find out how our sex-role behavior has been influenced by our culture, we do not have to go beyond the apes or monkeys to find almost anything we are looking for. We find some groups of apes which are predominantly monogamous, we find others which are polygamous, and still others which engage occasionally in homosexuality. There are also different dominance and aggression patterns. In some species it is the strongest and most aggressive male who is the dominant and most respected member of the group. In other species, in the Japanese Macaques, for example, it is not necessarily the most aggressive animal who is the dominant one. Eaton's (1976) observations suggest that certain males gain respect and dominance through the carry over of their mothers' influence. Only the sons of the high-ranking females are allowed to stay in the center of the troop where they learn bluff and self-confidence. Temperament differences between the apes have also been observed. The gorillas, for instance, are generally more docile and placid than the exuberant and excitable chimpanzees.

Basic to all cross-species comparisons is the question whether any behavior which an animal exhibits is natural; be it polygamy, monogamy, homosexuality, or the rejection of offsprings. Behavioral data from animals are extremely interesting, but for cross-species comparisons they can at best be used as hypotheses. Their validation will ultimately depend on experiments with humans.

Approaches to Equalization

We have outlined the subject matter of sex-role psychology and some of its experimental methods. We have also mentioned that the interest in a Psychology of Women and a Psychology of Sex-Roles have been stimulated by women's liberation groups striving for equality. Different liberation groups, however, advocate different approaches to equality. It will be useful to examine these approaches as each of them may require more-or-less different psychological orientations from both females and males. From the writings of female liberationists and from reports by professional and popular journals it appears that several equalization approaches have crystallized.

The earliest and major efforts of the women's emancipation movement have been directed towards the "masculinization" of women. The suffragists at the turn of the century demanded voting rights and access to jobs that men had reserved for themselves. Masculinization was again a central point in Betty Friedan's *The Feminine Mystique* (1963), a major work in the revival of the women's movement half a century later. It was Friedan's contention that in order to become creative and independent, women can free themselves from stifling and frustrating housework by integrating themselves into the masculine business world, by obtaining the best education, and by competing for the best jobs.

A controversial issue in the masculinization approach is the degree of dependency on male cooperation. After a decade of striving, the success of masculinization has been dubious. Friedan, who in 1966 was one of the founders of the National Organization for Women (NOW) was instrumental in forming in 1975 the splinter group, Womansurge. Friedan believes that the masculinization efforts of NOW are too direct and provocative. Lesbian rights, sex, and radical rhetoric are overstressed factors, creating resentment and noncooperation among male politicians and industrialists. The main task of Womansurge is to build coalitions on such "bread-and-butter" issues as more jobs for women, more day-care centers, and more opportunities for legal protection and advice (*Time*, Dec. 1975).

Merle Goldberg (1975), director of the National Women's Health Coalition, believes that the women's movement has lost part of its impact and leadership in the United States since the legalization of abortion has satisfied many women. The remaining and unfulfilled issues of equal work and equal pay do not generally receive the type of sympathy conducive to creating a "fighting spirit." Goldberg also believes that the failure of the American movement is directly related to the exclusion of men. The success of the masculinization efforts depends perhaps most on the existing economic conditions. It is difficult, even impossible, for women to obtain jobs held by men in times when both males and females are laid off or when new hiring has come to a standstill.

Another approach to equalization opposed to masculinization is "feminization." Virginia Woolf suggested feminization with the title character of her novel, *Orlando* (1928), although in reality the origin of this approach is difficult to discern. In general this approach, which advocates that males become more docile and more interested in child care and housework, is emphasized by women who are against masculinization; they believe that women should not copy male aggressiveness, but that males should change to less competitive and more relaxed business and work practices. A four-hour work day, for example, would increase employment and would make men less competitive. Additionally, it is hoped that males will become more docile and more reluctant to engage in war and crime. To a certain degree the feminization of men has also been advocated by women in support of masculinization, because more men will be needed for household work and child rearing once women are in full competition with males, and once their representation in the labor force is equally strong.

The feminization of men has not been too popular. It is estimated that only 10,000 children of a total of 6,000,000 born in the United States in 1975 experience solo fathering, although the number of older children who live with their fathers and without their mothers is much larger. Some success of the feminization movement has occurred in an increase in male child-care personnel and in the publication of how-to-do-it books on fathering such as

Father Power by Biller & Meredith (1974) and *What's a Father For?* by Sara Gilbert (1975). It is quite possible that the feminization approach will gain impetus with high male unemployment. A pilot program in New York sponsored by the Welfare Recipients Action Group, Inc., provides "surrogate fathers" who care for children during the day in fatherless homes (*Time,* Sept. 1975).

Another way to reach equalization is through "androgyny." The term "androgyny" comes from *andr* (man) and *gyne* (woman) and is used in biology to describe flowers bearing both stamenate and pistillate parts; it means in general both feminine and masculine. In contrast to both masculinization and feminization, androgyny does not require of either man or woman a total and exclusive acceptance of the sex-role traits characteristic of the opposite sex. Both sexes maintain their typical traits but incorporate also the traits of the opposite sex into their behavior repertoires. Thus, both men and women should be assertive and submissive, cautious and adventurous, dependent and independent, etc.

Nancy Bayley and Leona Bayer (1946) developed a scale to assess "somatic androgyny" by presenting pictures of the backsides of naked adults to raters, who would classify them into hypermasculine, masculine, bisexual, asexual, feminine, and hyperfeminine categories. Later, Bayley (1951) examined some psychological correlates of somatic androgyny and found that the body type had little influence of the subjects' psychological development, for instance, on the masculinity or femininity of expressed interests or preferences.

In the 1960s the meaning of the term "androgyny" seems to have changed to cover only psychological factors, implying ideally a zero difference between the sex stereotypes of men and women. Kate Millett (1971) recommends the male's clear and intellectual thinking and the female's gentleness and perceptiveness to both sexes. She believes that androgyny would be a desirable end-result, but that it can only be achieved after the monogamous and patriarchal family has been destroyed and only when females have complete sexual freedom and financial independence. Only then will male aggressiveness and female submissiveness have lost their usefulness. Sandra Bem (1975) envisions the androgynous individual as being less restrained by conventional sex-roles, and as being more flexible and freer to engage in whatever seems most effective at the moment. Bem cites various psychologists (Gall, 1969; Sears, 1970) who have found that high femininity in females has been consistently correlated with high anxiety and low self-esteem and that high masculinity in males correlates with neuroticism in adult males (Harford et al., 1967; Mussen, 1961). She believes that androgyny would also remedy these maladjustments.

Though androgyny is often recommended, details about its mode and consequences have not been worked out. It may be relatively simple to train a person to be both "intellectual" and "gentle" but teaching the acquisition of such opposing traits as aggression and submission may be much more problematical. It may lead to frustration and inactivity unless additional guidelines are given, guidelines that tell the individual when to be aggressive and when to be submissive. A more detailed treatment of the meaning and measurement of androgyny is presented in Chapter 8.

We may wonder which characteristics will be possessed by the ideal androgynous individual. Which characteristics will be chosen from the extremes and which from the average values? The average or norm is not always that which is most desired. The preference for the physical characteristics of hair color, for instance, fall at the two extremes, blond and black. The colors in between, which are more frequent, tend to be less admired and are sometimes called "dishwater blond," "mousy brown," etc. When it comes to the size of men, women prefer one end of the distribution, tallness. In facial features people prefer regularity and average sizes. Short and long noses are not so well liked as medium ones, but there are exceptions again, such as large eyes in women. Physical characteristics are much easier to define than psychological ones, but even here there are difficulties of establishing general norms. For psychological characteristics there are neither adequate definitions nor adequate norms, which makes androgyny an interesting, but a very speculative venture.

In the early 1970s a direction developed in the women's movement that can be entitled *womanhood.* On the order of "womanhood is beautiful," the movement emphasizes such womanly qualities as fertility and the importance of the woman's role in the child-rearing process. It is argued that women can become emancipated by recognizing their importance and that they can achieve equal status, equal pay, and equal satisfaction by doing what is typically female and not by doing that which is feministic—emulating men through masculinization or androgyny. Child bearing and child rearing, with all their accompanying tasks are considered virtuous whether or not they receive male support.

Such ideas are of course contrary to many advocates of women's liberation. Simone de Beauvoir recommends the opposite—getting away from the myth of motherhood and the motherhood instinct. Women, she believes, must rid society of these beliefs by refusing to do housework and by refusing to have children. Gloria Steinem considers the emphasis on womanhood a setback to the emancipation movement and Rita Mae Brown in the United States and Alice Schwarzer in Germany believe that the womanhood movement constitutes a direct counteroffensive (*Der Spiegel,* 1975).

Although the approaches suggested by the womanhood movement are quite different from other approaches, the final goals are similar. It may be possible that the womanhood movement will have success in obtaining payment for pregnancy, child care, and housework. In a market economy it is more advantageous to spread the news that one's work is important and unique than to say that it is monotonous and that anybody can do it.

Certain socialistic groups see the exploitation of women as only one consequence of the many oppressions capitalism creates and they believe that Marxism is the answer to female and male equality. Engels believed that the establishment of the patriarchal and monogamous family served capitalism by making it possible for property to pass from father to son. This fostered accumulation of property and as a consequence the exploitation of labor. It also made the woman financially and sexually dependent on one man. Marx, Bebel, Lenin, and other Marxist writers condemn the family and envision the liberation of women by integrating them into the economy so they could produce for the benefit of society. This aim was to be accomplished primarily through industrialization, in order to minimize the importance of physical strength. In that way female productivity could equal the productivity of males. Ironically, capitalism—especially the American brand—has most thoroughly replaced human labor by machine work so that in the 1970s we experience a surplus of both male and female labor.

Although the Marxists agreed that women should be fully integrated into the work force and freed from financial dependence on their husbands, from child-rearing tasks, and from household duties, they did not agree on the nature of their sexual relationships. Engels and Bebel supported "free love," while Lenin was for a monogamic relationship (Madden, 1972), and in the China of Mao Tse-tung (and his successors) sex and marriage are to be delayed until individuals are in their late twenties.

Modern Marxist views hold that capitalism creates competition that makes men struggle against men. In spite of this struggle many husbands cannot adquately support their families and they become dependent on the wife's supplemental income. The woman, being less skilled and having less seniority, will have to compete even harder than a man, while at the same time her entry into the labor market creates more competition for the man. This circular pitting of men against women is possible because capitalism supports the accumulation of private property, which allows temporary halts in production and employment and a dictation of wages. It is believed that the inequality of woman is caused by the economics of capitalism and not by any innate or acquired suppressive desires of males nor by any submissive urges of females.

Socialist trends in the women's movement seem to be more prevalent in Europe than in the United States. Some West German writers (Kunstmann, 1973) consider the following points as essential conditions for female equality: (1) Qualified training for all women; (2) A voice in determining the policy of the factory or firm; (3) Equal pay for equal work; (4) Infant-care and child-care centers and all-day schools; (5) Free access to medically supervised birth control; and (6) Legalized abortion (a demand that was turned down by the West German supreme court in 1975). In principle these demands are not much different from those made by the American liberation movement with the exception that the U.S. liberationists in general suggest payment for the distribution of goods and services through tax legislation, while the socialists advocate the abandonment of all property.

It may be an oversimplification to categorize female emancipation aims into "movements" as has been attempted in the previous pages. Jo Freeman (1975), discussing the origins of the women's liberation movement, recognizes two distinct origins: an "older" reform movement advocating women's rights and a "younger" radical movement advocating women's liberation. This younger group has proliferated through diverse local groups avoiding formal structure and works more on a person-to-person basis. This style, Freeman believes, has furthered personal change and flexibility but is politically less effective. As the two most important events of the movement Freeman (1973) mentions Betty Friedan's book, *The Feminine Mystique* and the addition of the word "sex" to Title VII of the 1964 U.S. Civil Rights Act.

A still different analysis of the aims of female liberation has been made by Rosemarie Nave-Herz (1975) and her collaborators who examined 221 German publications pertaining to female liberation. They divided all liberation demands into the following five basic categories: (1) Right to work; (2) Equal education; (3) Making actual use of work and educational rights; (4) Changes in socialization; and (5) Changes in family, school, and sexual matters. These categories are broadly defined and overlap in many respects. Nave-Herz comments that there is much agreement on the desire for change, but that exact definitions and the concrete suggestions on how to accomplish these changes are lacking. This indicates that the German movement described by Nave-Herz shows a similar proliferation as the "younger" U.S. movement examined by Freeman. Nave-Herz's more detailed analysis showed that 33 per cent of the books and articles she examined advocate changes in family and professions and that 27 per cent asked for changes in educational policies. Even more specifically, 16 per cent asked for family support through day care, kindergarten, and all-day schools, and 9 per cent advocated the total elimination of the family structure.

Since discrimination against females occurs in many facets of our daily lives—varying much in quantity and quality—it is not suprising that there is the variety of equalization approaches discussed above. Various approaches will require various ways to eliminate sex-role stereotypy and to establish new codes of conduct by which the sexes interact. Changes in the law and in the economy are often ineffective because underlying habits, attitudes, and interests remain unchanged. Thus the success of any equalization approach will depend much on these psychological variables. Their development and the feasibility of their modification will be discussed in the following chapters.

Chapter 2

HEREDITY AND ENVIRONMENT

Biological or innate differences have often been considered as logical and justified causes for the differential treatment of the sexes, but they have also been considered as illogical and unjustified by those who have experienced discrimination. It is the purpose of this chapter to discuss historically the hereditary and the environmental views on sex-role differences and to enumerate the biological sex differences existing at birth as well as those that develop during the growth process. An attempt will also be made to examine the interaction between biological and cultural factors with respect to female and male differences.

Three Views

One can find three general viewpoints on the heredity-environment issue with regard to sex differences. The "hereditary" view holds that men and women are born with distinctly different features and different psychological makeups and are thus destined to fulfill different and specific life tasks. Many religions that give women a subordinate role support the hereditary view. Buddhism considers rebirth in the form of a woman to be a punishment, and Islamic customs give women few rights in marital relationships. Paul specifically forbids women to rule over men, apparently leaving the way open for Christian men to rule over women. Not all religions, however, considered women to be inferior. The Teutons, for instance, ascribed visionary and godlike powers to women because they could create life.

Various philosophers have supported the hereditary view, most notably Schopenhauer, who believed that man was endowed by nature with all possible virtues and woman with all possible vices. Freud also viewed the sex differences as hereditary but did not relate them to mores or religion. He postulated that biologically innate and unconscious sexual urges permeate our conscious lives, affecting men and women differently in their daily strivings. More specifically he postulated that a woman's clitoris is an undeveloped penis; and that a woman's personality is unstable in many respects because she feels inferior, being envious of the man's sexual parts. The hereditary view propagated by many theologians, philosophers, and by Freud has generally been a view which has represented the sexes as unequal and women as inferior.

Opposed to the hereditary view is the "environmental" view, which holds that sex differences other than the obvious anatomical ones are socially learned, being entirely a product of culture. Such an extreme environmentalist position was advanced by Margaret Mead in 1935. In her well known book *Sex and Temperament in Three Primitive Societies* she describes three New Guinea tribes which were quite different with respect to their feminine and masculine characteristics. In the Arapesh tribe both men and women exhibited "feminine" traits, both being cooperative, gentle, and nonaggressive. Mead observed the opposite in the Mundugumor tribe, where both men and women were equally aggressive and competitive. In a third tribe, the Tchambuli, sex-roles were reversed, with the women engaging in fishing, trade, and production and men in the arts and in other nonutilitarian endeavors. Mead concludes that the characteristics of males and females in any society are solely conditioned by social customs and are not dependent upon biological inheritance. Mead's observational methods have been criticized by Piddington (1957), who believes that her sample was too small and her method biased. Murdock (1949) examined over 200 different cultures and found that in almost all of them men did the hunting and fishing and women the cooking and flour grinding.

In spite of the slim anthropological evidence in its favor the environmentalist view has been constantly gaining support. Simone de Beauvoir (1951) asserts that newborns of both sexes have equal experiences and interests, experience equal pleasures, and show equal amounts of passivity and activity. She believes that any sex differences in the above characteristics that may appear later must be entirely a matter of learning. Kate Millett in her book *Sexual Politics* (1971) states that "psychosexual" differences are learned. This would mean that our sexual thoughts, desires, and feelings, inasmuch as they are included in the definition of "psychosexual", are learned and are not influenced by those chemicals and hormones of which female and male bodies produce different types and amounts.

The third viewpoint may be called the "interaction" view since it describes a dependent relationship between heredity and environment. This viewpoint has not been advocated as strongly as the strict hereditary and environmental views since it is a middle-of-the-road approach and since most researchers who propose it are unsure to which degree a certain trait is determined by heredity and to which degree it is influenced by environment.

The genetics of psychological traits are much more elusive than the heritability of diseases and other physiological data. They are difficult to assess for a present generation and the data are practically nonexistent for previous ones—data that would be necessary to determine genetic relationships. Another difficulty is the great variation which psychological traits show in their dependency on heredity. Cattell (1955) found that such personality factors as "tender-mindedness," "general neuroticism," and "will control" are predominantly environmentally conditioned and that such traits as "energetic conformity" and "dominance" depend in equal parts on heredity and environment, while heredity plays a greater role for traits related to "hyperactivity-depressions," "submissiveness," and "general intelligence."

Interaction can occur in several different ways. Infant boys, for instance, sleep one to two hours less per day than infant girls and are in general more active while they are awake. It has also been observed that mothers interact more often with newly born boys, holding them for longer periods and stressing their musculature more often (Moss, 1967). Mothers may do this in order to quiet their more active and more fussy boys, but in actuality it may have the opposite effect, since the additional physical and social contact may make the boys even more active. Whatever the reasons, the biologically more active organism elicits from his environment, usually his mother, a more active response. Here as in many other instances heredity and environment work together to amplify an originally given difference. This effect is called "co-variance," indicating that heredity varies and with it also the environmental conditions.

Throughout their lives women are slightly superior to men in dealing with verbal material. As discussed more detailed in the following chapter, girl infants vocalize more than boy infants soon after birth and parents talk more to girls than to boys during the first years of childhood. Nature and environment seem to complement each other and both may contribute to the verbal superiority of women. The effects of co-variance occur on all age levels. Because boys are more muscular than girls in adolescence, they are often given more opportunities to participate in sports that additionally strengthen their muscles. Co-variance can also be observed within one sex where boys with a naturally stronger body type receive frequently more training than weaker boys. The effects of co-variance can of course be reversed, but it usually takes special efforts or programs to further the weaker children in sports or the less intelligent ones in education.

Interaction occurs also without co-variance in situations where the environment is kept constant and were organisms differing in heredity are often sensitive to different aspects of their environment. For example, Heinstein (1963) found that boys and girls react differently to breast feeding and also to bottle feeding. Formula-fed boys show more bed-wetting than breast-fed boys, but have fewer fears and better appetites. Girls show opposite tendencies. Those being breast-fed have fewer fears, better appetites, and more bed-wettings. Thus interaction can work in two different ways. For example, because boys are more active by heredity, they may select more active toys from their environment even though they are given the same choices as girls (e.g., trucks and dolls). This type of interaction is called "simple interaction" because only one factor, the heredity one, varies. Secondly, because boys are more active by nature they are stimulated by their environment to play more with such activity toys as trucks. As already mentioned this type of interaction is called co-variance. Both types of interaction occur in the process of human development.

Physiological Differences

There are distinct differences in every cell of the female and male body, but the purpose or the function of some of these differences is not known. For example, in 1949 Barr and Bertram discovered sex chromatin, a chemical present in every cell of the female body but in no cell of the male body. As yet it is not known what the presence of sex chromatin does to the female body or what its absence implies for the male body. Male and female cells are also differentiated by the shape of one of the 23 pairs of chromosomes. The function of this chromosome pair is inferred from certain sex-linked diseases or conditions that occur in one sex but not in the other. Hemophilia (excessive bleeding) occurs only in men, color blindness is much more frequent among males than among females, and such conditions as autism (childhood schizophrenia), bed-wetting, stuttering, hyperactivity, and dyslexia are about five times as frequent among males as among females. Male fetuses are aborted more often than female ones and the infant mortality rate is higher for males than for females. The male has more health difficulties than the female, and that seems to hold true in general for all animals and humans in all cultures.

The reasons for the males' inferior physiological conditions are not known. It has been speculated, however, that the extra X in the female XX combination of her chromosomes gives her certain protections that the male XY combination does not afford the male. The female, for example, transmits hemophilia to her male offspring. She is genetically not "free" from hemophilia but seems to have an additional mechanism that prevents the occurrence of the disease—the actual bleedings. Among the children of a hemophilic father and a healthy mother all sons would be healthy, and all daughters would be carriers of hemophilia; while among the children of a healthy father and a carrier mother, half the boys would be hemophiliacs and half the daughters would be carriers. In addition, between 20 and 40 per cent of all hemophiliacs have no family history of it. Their condition is due to mutations in the sperm cells of the mother or of the mother's father (Steinhausen, 1976).

It is obvious that the conditions of hemophilia and color blindness are biologically determined and not influenced by environment. Neither can the higher rate of the aborting of males be influenced by the environment, since the sex of the fetus is generally not known until it is aborted. The biological determinants of such conditions as autism, stuttering, and bed-wetting are more difficult to ascertain. Normal children, for instance, do not speak during their first year of life nor do they read until they go to school and such difficulties as stuttering or dyslexia would not manifest themselves before their maturational periods have passed. This makes it difficult to factor out environmental effects and to attest that the environment had no influence. Only indirect evidence suggests that the above-mentioned disturbances are mainly biological in origin because in almost all cultures and subcultures more boys than girls experience these handicaps. The environment may have an ameliorating or a worsening effect on individual cases, but in general the male-female ratio of these handicaps is not influenced by social class, father absence, nor by any other socioeconomic conditions.

The X and Y chromosomes carry about five per cent of the total genetic material that a person inherits. This includes the obvious anatomical sex differences and some of the above-mentioned pathological conditions. The X-linkage concept (also called Lehrke's theory or Lyon's hypothesis) holds that in females the expression of any deviant member of a gene pair on one X chromosome is likely to be offset or modified by the other X on the female XX chromosome. As mentioned, this mechanism probably prevents the female from having the symptoms or the actual disease of hemophilia. It may also be responsible for the greater physiological and psychological stabilities females generally show. As will be discussed later (see Chapter 5) females are less influenced by their environment than are males. Males on the other hand deviate more among themselves, counting more idiots as well as more geniuses.

In females a recessive X-linked trait must occur in both X's, in the one inherited from the mother as well as in the one inherited from the father. In males, however, the trait needs to be represented in only one X chromosome, since they have only one X chromosome (the one they inherit from their mother). The likelihood that females will show an X-linked trait is the square of the proportion with which this trait occurs in males. This linkage concept fits the observed sex differences in color blindness. One in 20 males is color blind, but only one in 400 females is so afflicted.

From the female XX and the male XY combinations, the X-linkage theory predicts certain interesting within-family correlations. With respect to X-linked traits, fathers and sons should not be alike since the son does not inherit an X chromosome from his father. Father-daughter correlations should be higher than father-son correlations since the daughter inherits one X chromosome from her father. Further, father-daughter correlations should be higher than mother-daughter correlations because the father's X-linked trait will always be given to the daughter (as in hemophilia: All daughters of a hemophilic father will be carriers); while the mother's X-linked trait will only be given to half her sons or daughters since she has two X chromosomes, of which only one is transmitted to her offspring (as in hemophilia: Only half the daughters and half the sons have hemophilia if the mother is a carrier and the father is healthy).

It is still a question whether any personality or mental traits (and if so, which ones) are transmitted by the five per cent sex-linked inheritance. Michele Andrisin Wittig (1976) has reviewed the literature on the inheritance of the ability to visualize space. Three separate studies she cites suggest that this trait is inherited because the results of the studies showed the above-mentioned within-family correlation that a recessive X-linkage theory would predict. Wittig points out that the spatial-visual ability tested in the various experiments was of a specific kind and that there is no evidence that the X-linkage hypothesis can be applied to the IQ or any other mental function. She mentions further that there is much overlap between the sexes in spite of the higher male averages and that these higher male scores do not contradict an environmental or learning hypothesis. Few psychological traits have been examined as to their X-linkage possibility. Such investigations are cumbersome. They require reliable tests, data on parents and children, as well as same-sex and cross-sex comparisons.

There are a number of physiological differences apparent at birth and thereafter that may or may not influence the way females and males think and act. At birth, for instance, girl infants have more subcutaneous fat (Stolz & Stolz, 1951) yet they are more sensitive to pain and tactual stimulation (Lipsitt & Levy, 1959; Bell & Costello, 1964). Height remains equal for both sexes until age seven when girls become slightly taller than boys. This difference is maintained until age ten when boys become taller than girls. By adulthood males are 6 per cent taller and 20 per cent heavier than females (Jackson & Kelly, 1945). Girls mature faster than boys. Their skeletal development at birth is four weeks in advance of boys and at adolescence three years in advance (Eichorn, 1968). At puberty girls have a higher pulse rate (2–6 beats per min.) while boys begin to show an increase in blood pressure. The male blood has about 300,000 more red blood corpuscles per cubic millimeter (Nash, 1970) and from adolescence the blood pressure after exercise begins to increase in boys and to decrease in girls. It has been postulated by Shock (1971) that these physiological conditions may influence sex differences in athletics.

Other changes occur during puberty that increase the dissimilarity between males and females. Males begin to have a higher metabolic rate (about 20 per cent higher), produce more physical energy, and require more food. From age 13 their Recommended Daily Allowances (RDA) for energy and protein is about 25 per cent more than the RDA for females. Only during pregnancy and lactation are the requirements for women equal to those for men (for some foods they are higher then). Males also need more thiamine, riboflavin, and niacin; but for the vitamins A, C, and D the needs for males and females are equal. Iron seems to be the only nutrient of which women from age 13 require about twice as much as men (Scrimshaw & Young, 1976).

Additional anatomical sex differences occur during puberty. In males there is an initial swelling of the mammary gland, the growth of pubic and facial hair, and the appearance of the Adam's apple and the voice break. These changes, called secondary sex characteristics, occur during the years 13 to 17, with the strongest growth at 14. They occur as a consequence of an increased testosterone level, which remained unchanged during the years from 3 to 9; but as already mentioned the level increases tenfold during the years from 10 to 15. In females the growth peak is reached at age 12 with breast and pelvis enlargement, the appearance of pubic hair, and the onset of menstruation occurring between the ages 11 to 15 (Tanner, 1962).

The pubertal changes are a consequence of hormonal secretions, androgen or testosterone in males and estrogen in females. Infants produce relatively small quantities of sex hormones, but both sexes produce testosterone and estrogen. Testosterone is known as the male hormone because males produce it in much larger quantities than females; estrogen is known as the female hormone because females produce more of it than males. In females estrogen is secreted by the ovaries acting specifically on tissues associated with the vagina, the uterus, the oviducts, and the breasts. In males testosterone secreted by the testes acts specifically on the seminal vesicle and the prostate gland. The sex hormones act also on the brain to stimulate sex-differentiated behavior. As described by McEwen (1976), there are special cells, or "target neurons," in the brain that are genetically modified by these sex hormones. In humans the modification of these target neurons seems to occur sometimes early in fetal life whereby more permanent neural reaction patterns are established, which in turn determine the more or less fixed sexual responses. Once these circuits are formed their basic structure may no longer be susceptible to hormonal influences, although the hormone can still signal to the brain cells whether or not and to which degree they should act. This may relate to the clinical observations that humans increase or decrease their sexual behaviors under high or low hormonal levels without essential changes in their response patterns.

It is not known how chemically the target neurons bring about the various sexual behaviors. Paradoxically, it has been found that the testosterone that reaches the target neurons of the male brain is transformed into the female hormone endrogen by an enzyme within these male neurons. The female hormone seems to be the stimulus for both the female and the male target neurons. Animal experiments have also shown that the male brain will retain a female response pattern if testosterone is prevented from reaching the target neurons by early castration or by other means. There are still many unknowns in the cycle in which the hormones of the brain stimulate the production of the sex hormones in the gonads, and in which these hormones in turn form as well as activate neuronal target cells that send the final impulses to the muscles and glands involved in sexual behavior. Sexual behavior is often linked to energy states and moods controlled by steroid hormones secreted by the adrenal cortex, which has its own cyclical relationship with neurons in the brain. This linkage makes the investigation of pure sexual behavior even more difficult.

Behavioral Differences

The gender differences reported above were differences in cell structure, weight, heart rate, blood pressure, etc. In most cases their functional purpose was unknown or at best an educated guess. Conversely, we know various behavioral or functional gender differences but have little knowledge of their underlying physiology. For example, right after birth boys are more active, sleep less, and stretch and raise their heads higher and for longer periods than girl infants (Bell & Darling, 1965). Girls sleep longer, move their mouths more often, and vocalize more. Other behavioral differences occur later and are probably strongly influenced by cultural stereotypes. Yet they occur with a certain regularity at specific ages during male and female development and the possibility of a biological origin should be considered.

Psychologists have often postulated that certain learning capacities are innate, but their postulates have been criticized because they have often assessed these capacities or potentials—such as the IQ years after birth—when there was ample chance for environmental influences. There are, however, some learning or conditioning tasks that have been given to neonates hours after birth where the environment had practically no chance to interact. Their results suggest that there are learning differences at birth. Stamps and Porges (1975) tested the heart rate conditioning of infants as early as 40 to 75 hours after birth. They presented a tone as a signal or cue and a few seconds later a series of blinking, colored lights suspended over the neonate's crib to effect changes in heart rate. Only the females among their subjects showed a decrease of the heart rate and a decrease in sucking response after they had experienced the pairings of tone and light. The authors suggest that females have an innately higher level of attention and responsiveness.

The results of the above experiment may relate to the finding that female infants are more receptive to auditory stimuli and that boy infants learn better when visually stimulated. Watson (1969) reinforced ten-week-old infants with tones and visual figures for fixating a particular special position and found that the girl infants learned with the tone but not with the visual reinforcement; conversely, the boy infants learned with the visual but not with the auditory reward. In another experiment, however, it was found that female infants did learn when the visual reward was an illuminated checkerboard design which was activated by the infants own sucking motions. Adele Franks and Keith Berg (1975) found that females increased their sucking rate to 56 times per observation period (2 minutes), while the males remained at their preexperimental base rate of 38 times. Although the authors state that females "clearly and significantly" incremented their response rate whereas the males remained at baseline level, they are reluctant to ascribe these differences to a difference in learning since they used no control group in their experiment. Yet without the learning hypothesis it is difficult to explain why the females increased their sucking rate after the introduction of the reward.

Not all experimenters who tested neonates found sex differences in learning, and there are seeming conflicts in the experiments discussed above with Watson reporting that his female infants did not learn under visual reward conditions, while Franks & Berg found that only the females and none of the male infants changed their responses when visually stimulated. It should be noted that the result of a learning experiment depends often on what appears to be a minor detail in the stimulating situation. The visual stimulus used by Watson consisted of two red circles with eyes, eyebrows, and a curved mouth, while Franks and Berg used an illuminated checkerboard. In general, learning experiments with neonates are difficult to conduct because the infant subjects must be awake and should be dry, calm, and attentive—conditions not too readily found with the newborn. Also their behavior repertoire is limited to such responses as heart rate, sucking, head turning, and arm and leg reflexes—responses difficult to condition because they show much variation and spontaneous fluctuations independent of conditioning.

Aggression

It is often suggested that a good part of the sex-role inequality stems from male aggression manifesting itself in the suppression of females through warfare, politics, sexual practices, and through competition in education, business, and industry. Much has been written about the aggressive nature of man, and here again it was Freud who postulated that aggression is an innate, biological drive—a drive responsible for self-inflicted pain, sadism, and self-destruction. In a letter to Einstein discussing the prevention of wars Freud reiterated that destruction satisfies an instinctual desire and that it would be futile to attempt to eliminate aggression. He believed that aggression underlies a basic death instinct, which he termed "Thanatos," opposed to forces of the life instinct, which he called "Eros." Somewhat more hopefully, Freud conceded that aggression can be modified, although not eliminated, by strengthening the Eros instinct through forming emotional ties with others.

The view that aggression is genetic became popular again in the 1960s through the writings of the German ethologist Konrad Lorenz (Selg, 1974). From observing animals he concluded that aggression is natural and functional because it spreads animals over a wider area giving them larger feeding grounds, and because it creates a stronger species through the survival of the fittest. Lorenz does not consider that aggression would not serve those animals who need to live in herds in order to protect themselves from other animals and that it makes little difference to the survival of any species whether it is thinned out by its own aggressive members or by its natural enemies. Lorenz contends further that instinctual aggression has lost its functional value for humans. They overkill because they fight with weapons that eliminate direct confrontation with the enemy and prevent the association between aggression and pain. Thus in comparison to animals humans have fewer chances of learning to inhibit their aggression. In this respect Lorenz's view of aggression is not entirely instinctual but follows some aspects of learning principles. Leaving Freud's and Lorenz's speculations aside there are many observational data that suggest that aggression is innate in many animal species. In animals, male aggression involves most often the act of copulation and the defense of sex mates. As early as 1849 it was shown by Berthold that castrated roosters no longer crowed, fought, or exhibited sexual behavior. After Berthold implanted testis tissue into the abdominal cavity of the rooster the masculine activities reappeared. This experiment was one of the first to demonstrate the presence of a hormone—a substance reaching the brain through the blood and not dependent on neuronal connections.

Many other animal experiments have repeatedly shown that aggression can be increased by raising an animal's male hormone level. Hens low on the pecking order (being pecked by all other hens) can move to the top of the pecking order (pecking, but not being pecked by the other hens) if given the male hormone, testosterone. This upward mobility can also be obtained through the feeding of

extra vitamins and other nutrients. It has also been reported that female cancer patients who received large
doses of male hormones for therapeutic purposes experienced increased sexual urges.

Archer (1975) has cautioned against accepting animal
data to explain human aggressiveness by hormonal differences and Bandura (1973) also points out that experiments
investigating human aggressiveness and its relationship to
testosterone and to the abnormality of the double XYY
chromosome have shown uncertain results. Humans as
compared to animals are much less dependent on instincts,
fixed neural patterns, or hormones. Injections of testosterone will generally cause aggression and sexual behavior in
lower animals. In animals higher on the phylogenetic scale,
the relationship between testosterone and aggression is
not as clear. It has been shown that testosterone can influence their behavior, but their behavior can also determine
their testosterone output. For example, male rhesus monkeys that have been subjected to defeat by dominant males
show a distinct decrease in testosterone. When these de-
feated males were exposed to female companions their testosterone level returned quickly to normal (McEwan,
1976). If there are any genetic and sex-specific factors that
cause human aggression, they seem to be subordinate to
environmental influences. A number of experiments on
imitation that relate aggression to social learning will be
discussed in Chapter 4.

General activity has often been related to aggression
although one can be active without being aggressive, especially if one directs his activities towards certain tasks in
play and sports that are socially not considered aggressive.
This leads to the question of whether boys are genetically
more active than girls, and there are a number of observations and experiments that indicate that there is a slight
difference. It has already been pointed out that boys sleep
less in early infancy and that the disturbance of hyperac-

tivity is five times as frequent in boys as in girls. On the preschool level boys have been found repeatedly more active, exploratory, bullying, and more aggressive in play (Goldberg & Lewis, 1969; Maccoby & Jacklin, 1971). With regard to motor activities, Jenkins (1930) and Gutteridge (1939) observed that boys are slightly more proficient in most gross motor skills: in tricycling, hopping, bouncing, and ball catching. These results, however, seem to depend on the age level at which comparisons are made. Govatos (1959) found that females at age six are better than boys in the standing broad jump and in the 25-yard dash, but that these differences even out again at age ten. During adolescence boys begin to outperform girls in almost all athletic activities. Ausubel (1954) describes the physical bases for the increase in activity and lists the growth of muscular tissue caused by androgenic stimulation and the increase in cardiac capacity as main factors.

All in all the above studies indicate that boys are more active in their preschool years and again during and after adolescence. Between the ages from 6 to 10 the activity levels of boys and girls seem to be equal. These observations suggest that the biological growth can also influence behavior because the boys' lead should continue through the middle years of childhood if we assume that the cultural stereotype is the sole factor in the boys' increased activity. It is unlikely that the cultural sex-role stereotypes influence boys differently in the preschool years than they do in the early school years. Conversely we may ask if girls were taught in early childhood to be quiet and inactive, why their activity level is equal to—and at times superior to—boys during the ages from 6 to 10. Such a comparison of the activity of boys and girls fits the biological growth curves. During the middle years of childhood when girls equal or excel in growth, differences in motor activities disappear, but became apparent again after age 10 when the boys' growth begins to accelerate.

An attempt has been made to examine the fantasies of verbal and play activity of children between the ages of 5 and 11 by Phebe Cramer and Katherine Hogan (1975). They report that the themes of the boys' fantasies consist of "rising and falling," "danger and violence," and "exterior action," while the fantasies of girls are characterized by "ornamental, intruding, and interior" action. Though the authors cite no cross-cultural controls they conclude mainly from the similarity of the responses which they obtained from their subjects that not all the sex differences in fantasy can be attributed to social learning and that their inner feelings are partly based on biological differences. Conversely, one could argue that cultural stereotypes remain constant and that the very similarity between the results of 5 to 11-year-olds supports the social learning theory.

DISCUSSION

A number of biological differences between females and males have been enumerated. Some exist at birth, others arise during the maturational process, and some remain with us throughout our lives influencing our health and even the difference in male and female longevity. While many biological sex differences can be recognized, their functional purposes remain often unknown. For example, the observations that male infants are more active, that they have more red blood cells, more testosterone, etc., do not allow us to reach any conclusions about the boys' more pronounced aggressiveness. Since the environment interacts constantly (in supporting as well as in inhibiting ways) with our innate capacities and potentialities and since environment on the human level cannot be held constant, we can only determine through indirect ways to what degree genetic and environmental factors are responsible for the psychological sex differences as they exist in our culture. Although the evidence is indirect, the influence of biology has been shown by comparing the physical growth of boys and girls with their activities in sports. The biology plays also a predominate part in the susceptibility to certain diseases and in the life-span differences which exist between females and males.

Overall statements about the influence of heredity can only be made about general predispositions or drive levels but not about specific behaviors. The biology seems to furnish certain initial predispositions and urges (e.g., our hunger) while the environment determines the ways we will satisfy these urges (e.g., what we will eat). For an adolescent the biology makes it possible to become sexually stimulated; however, the specific object for this stimulation and the mode of satisfaction will be largely determined by the culture and by the individual's specific environment.

Judging by certain physiological measures, females are at birth maturationally more advanced than boys and they keep this advance until puberty. The learning experiments cited in this chapter indicate that at birth it is the female who is more responsive and attentive in learning situations. Yet it is not known how much this initial difference contributes to the differential treatment females receive from their parents, who have the tendency to talk to their female offsprings more often than to their male ones. Neither is it known how much the learning differences at birth and early childhood contribute to the female's inclination to learn verbal materials more readily than nonverbal matters as compared to males who show a reverse tendency.

Biological sex differences have become more and more unimportant with advances in industrialization and medical technology. The child-bearing capacity of females has lost much of its functional value as far as the survival of the human race is concerned. In developed countries present population figures can be maintained if most women have two children, while at the turn of the century a woman needed to give birth to six children for the birth rate to equal the death rate. For males and females alike it has become financially more rewarding and economically more productive to make one's living more with one's wits than with one's brawn. In the distant past it may have been important for the survival of the human species that the division of labor took place along biological lines. When survival was at stake and utmost energies were needed men did the hunting and plowing and women bore children and reared them. A division of labor based on biological suitability does by no means necessitate an unequal status between man and woman. Judith Blake (1974) believes that the woman's dependency, or her derived status, was primarily conditioned by the industrial revolution with men working in factories and women working at home—with men being paid and women not.

Speculations and facts about the inborn nature of sex differences come from a number of disciplines, such as anthropology, sociology, psychology, and physiology. It is generally believed that innate traits are unchangeable and that it is "bad" or unfair to investigate or talk about them. People feel much more comfortable with an acquired or learned trait, even if it is bad, because they assume that learned traits can be changed more readily than inborn ones. There is much evidence against such "comforting" notions. For example, neither the psychologists who believe that the IQ is mainly a matter of environment, nor those who believe it is mainly a matter of heredity, have had much success raising IQ's durably and substantially. There are other behaviors, mainly acquired, such as drinking, smoking, speeding, and overeating that have been rather resistant to environmental influences. Could it be that the geneticist or the physiologist will invent a pill before the psychologist discovers successful methods to accomplish behavioral changes?

The question of heredity and environment becomes less important if we are primarily concerned with sex-role changes. Certain innate traits or desires can be more readily changed than other acquired ones. Most parents are successful in toilet training their children, although the desire for a child to urinate whenever and wherever the urge is felt is something very much innate. For the child, toilet training may be quite unnatural. Aggression or trait X could be innate and yet we may successfully countercondition it if we start at birth. Conversely, aggression or trait X could be learned, yet we may not be successful in counterconditioning if we start at adolescence or later. The degree to which a behavior is innate or acquired does not necessarily determine the ease or the difficulty with which it can be modified. An inborn tendency of the females to be more verbal and of the males to be more active and spatially oriented could readily be compensated—or even overcompensated—by the environment, thereby creating a society in which women are more active and men more verbal. Thus our incomplete knowledge about the origin of certain sex-linked traits or behaviors should not discourage us from modifying them if the change is to the benefit of society.

Chapter 3

DEVELOPMENT AND SEX-ROLES

Whatever heredity and environment may contribute to our
sex-roles, the fact remains that they become imbedded in
our personalities. We rarely know how they and our entire
self-image as members of the female or male sex became
established. From birth we interact daily with people and
objects in our environment, and sex-roles can be formed
on innumerable occasions with varying degrees of subtlety.
In this chapter we shall attempt to discern which specific
sex-roles differences exist at various developmental periods and, if possible, in which mode and to what degree they
become established through parents, teachers, and peers.

Infancy

Parents seem to sex-type their infants on the first day they
are born. Rubin et al. (1974) asked 30 pairs of parents of
one-day-old infants to describe them as they would to a
close friend or relative. Fifteen of the parent pairs were the

parents of boy infants, 15 of girl infants. The fathers only viewed the infants, but the mothers viewed and held them before they were asked to describe them. In actuality the boy and girl infants did not differ in their average birth weight, birth length, or in various medical indexes (Apgar score); yet they were differentially perceived and labeled. Both mothers and fathers described their daughters more often as little, beautiful, cute, weaker, delicate, and as resembling their mothers. Boys were described more often as firmer, larger featured, better coordinated, more alert, stronger, and hardier.

The actual viewing and holding of these babies could not have caused the differential description since the boys and girls were equal in body dimensions and activity level. One must conclude that the differential descriptions were based on preconceived notions of maleness and femaleness. In another study by Jerrie Ann Will et al. (1976) the same infant, a six-month-old boy, was presented to some mothers with blue pants under the name of "Adam" and to others with a pink dress by the name of "Beth." The mothers were asked to hold the infant and to play with him or her for several minutes. All mothers had small children of both sexes of their own. Most of them reported that they perceived no differences in the actions of male and female infants and that they encouraged roughhouse play with their own daughters and doll play with their sons. Yet in the experimental situation they handed a doll, which was in the experimental room, more often to "Beth" and a train, which was likewise present, more often to "Adam." They also smiled more often when they believed they were holding a female. None of the mothers seemed to be aware of this differential treatment. The above studies show that our stereotypes influence our perceptions of certain of the infants' physical dimensions, their behavioral traits, and our own actions toward the infants.

The interaction between parent and infant was also

studied by Freda Rebelsky and Cheryl Hanks (1971) who attached microphones to infants' shirts for 24-hour periods and found some striking results. Fathers interacted vocally with their newly born infants only 37 seconds per day! This vocalization time decreases during the first three months, and moreover it decreases more for girls than for boys. Thus, fathers spend very little time interacting with their newly born infants of both sexes, and even less time with their girl infants. While the father's interaction time decreases during the first three months, the mother's time was found to increase. Mothers with boy infants begin to talk to them less after the first three months, while mothers with girl infants begin to talk more and more often after this three-month period (Moss, 1967).

Various hypotheses have been advanced to explain these differences in the treatment of infants. Moss suggests that mothers respond initially more to their boy infants because they are awake longer and more active than girl infants. After several months, however, the mothers may get tired of talking to their more irritable boys, while the mothers of girls find it more pleasant to talk to them since girls have been reported as calmer and as more frequent vocalizers than boys. Moss's hypothesis follows the interactionist's view that the differential treatment is partially due to a biological disposition differing for boy and girl infants.

The mothers' initial and differential treatment of their boy infants may also be based on a general, cultural preference toward males and not on an interaction with biology. Mao Tse-tung, for instance, repeatedly told his American friend Edgar Snow (1971) that the greatest stumbling block toward reaching population zero growth is the Chinese woman's desire to have male offspring. Many women in China are reluctant to engage in birth control after their second child if the first two children are girls. The preferences of Americans with regard to the sex of their offspring are equally biased and resistant to change. Candida and

James Peterson (1973) asked future parents for the sex preference of their first and only child. They found that a boy was wanted by 90 per cent of the men and by 92 per cent of the women. They compared their results with a similar study conducted in 1954 when a boy was wanted by 93 per cent of the men and by 90 per cent of the women. No essential change over a period of 20 years!

A further differential treatment by fathers was reported by Rebelsky and Hanks (1971). They examined the times fathers engaged in caretaking (diapering, feeding) and in noncaretaking activities; they found that fathers interact with girl infants 62 per cent during caretaking and 38 per cent during noncaretaking. With boy infants their interaction is almost reverse with 34 per cent during caretaking and 66 per cent during noncaretaking. It seems that fathers relate caretaking to "mothering" and may feel that it is bad for a man to mother a female, but much worse to mother a male.

Considering the differential treatment infants receive from their two parents, it is understandable that the type and the quality of the interaction differs also. Peggy Ban and Michael Lewis (1974) investigated "attachment" behavior of one-year-olds. They observed boys and girls playing 15 minutes with their mothers and 15 minutes with their fathers. They found that both boys and girls spent about twice as much time in the proximity of their mothers as in the proximity of their fathers. They also touched their mothers about twice as often as their fathers. When attachment was measured by "looking" at a parent, it was found that boys looked about twice and girls equally as often at their fathers as at their mothers. One should expect by the laws of learning (association, habit—discussed in the following chapter) that the infants seek to continue with each parent the type of interaction to which they have become accustomed—touching and closeness with the mother, distal and looking with the father.

Several studies have shown that the father is a rather important figure for the child to model or imitate (see Chapter 4), in spite of his infrequent presence. One may wonder if it is his actual and relatively short presence that influences this modeling or whether his male image is portrayed through the mother ("Wait until Daddy comes home"), television, or other media. In an attempt to answer this question, Ban and Lewis correlated the time fathers spent at home with their children with the amount of attachment behavior shown by the children. They found that in their sample of upper-middle-class families the fathers spent an average of 15 to 20 minutes per day with their children, ranging from zero to two hours. (Some fathers who reported zero time said that the child is asleep when they return from work.) Somewhat surprisingly, Ban and Lewis found no correlation between the time of the father's home contact and the degree of the child's attachment. They suggest that this is due to the quality and not the quantity of the father-son interaction. Since this interaction may be stressful, a prolongation of it may work against attachment. Could it be that even our infants know that absence makes the heart grow fonder?

The above studies, which reported various differential treatments of boy and girl infants, did not investigate the parents' awareness of it. One can assume that many of the treatment differences at this early age are unintentional and that the parents are in general not aware of the incidents where they treat or react differently to boy and girl infants. Mothers, for instance, may be totally unaware that they talk longer to their three-month-old girls; neither may fathers be aware that they dislike mothering male infants. Most of us act in a given cultural and socioeconomic framework, with perhaps few reflections and few whys and wherefores to our daily child-rearing (or lack of child-rearing) activities.

Childhood and Play

The play of infants and children is considered a precursor of later activities and a number of psychologists have investigated it as an indicator and perhaps also as a cause of early sex-role differences. In a very detailed and thorough investigation McCall (1974) examined various manipulative and play behaviors of infants between 8 and 11 months old. He presented toys varying in configuration, plasticity, sound quality, and familiarity to both infants and mothers, and he observed the infant's selection preferences, length of playtime, and attention. He reported no consistent sex differences in the nature of play behavior, the toys played with, nor the infant's orientation toward the parent (mostly the mother) during play. At the 13- to 15-month level, McCall found males played more vigorously with mechanical and manipulative toys and girls more often with stuffed animals and cuddly toys, but these differences were small and dependent on specific toys.

There were earlier studies, notably the one by Susan Goldberg and Michael Lewis (1969). They reported that boys played more vigorously and that girls were more reluctant to give up contact with their mothers before and during play. These results have not been verified by McCall nor by Messer and Lewis (1972), and it appears that the differences found by Goldberg and Lewis depended on toy familiarity and on the selection of children from a specific socioeconomic level. At the upper socioeconomic levels, one could expect more parental training and possibly more opportunities for the transfer of cultural stereotypes.

Toy preferences seem to crystallize by the end of the second year. Observing two-year-olds in a nursery Claire Etaugh et al. (1975) found that girls were more likely than boys to paint, help the teacher, look at books, or listen to stories; boys preferred to hammer and to play with transportation toys. It was also observed that the boys had a larger range of selection, spending more time than the girls in the opposite sex activities. Similar results were observed by Greta Fein et al. (1975). In an experimental play situation they found that their 20-month-old girls contacted girl-toys (bracelet, doll, iron) more often than boy-toys (hammer, gun, truck), while the boys played with girl-toys and boy-toys equally often. Familiarity with a toy did not relate to the frequency with which it was contacted, since Fein et al. examined the children's home situation and found that girls had many boy-toys, but boys had few girl-toys. The range of contact reverses itself in the middle years of childhood when girls play more often with male and female toys while boys play rarely with sex-inappropriate toys. In a trend study, to be discussed in Chapter 9, Rosenberg and Sutton-Smith (1960) found that of 27 play activities considered as masculine in the 1930s 17 were considered as neutral in the 1960s—a trend that has widened the girls' play repertoire but not the boys'.

Beverly Fagot (1974) observed two-year-olds in their family environment interacting with their mother and father; she found also that toy preferences had been established by the age of two. Boys preferred to manipulate objects or toys, and girls preferred to play with soft toys and dolls. Girls also asked for help, danced, and dressed up in adult-like clothes more often. Fagot observed also the moods of the children while engaged in their play. Rating them on a 7-point scale from "extremely happy" to "extremely unhappy or mad" she found that there was no difference between the sexes. Both sexes were rated as cheerful 10 times more frequently than they were mad or unhappy. Although they play with different toys, two-year-olds seem to be equally happy, apparently not feeling any of the qualitative differences their parents or their observing psychologists may experience! The girls' happiness about their sex-role, however, does not last. Many girls in later childhood years wish they were boys rather than girls.

At the three-year-old level toy preferences are clear and distinct. McCandless and Evans (1973), who observed three-year-olds in a nursery, found that girls play about 90 per cent of the time at "girlish" activities, and boys play at "boyish" activities 90 per cent of the time.

As the above studies have shown, toy preferences are formed during a child's second year and show consistency during the third year. Several researches have examined the role parents and nursery school teachers play in establishing them. Observing in home situations, Fagot (1974) found that both parents gave girls more praise as well as more criticism and that they joined boys' play more actively than girls' play. Mothers gave more praise than fathers, but mothers also physically punished both sexes more than fathers. Observing also in family situations with children ranging between five and eight years, Gayla Margolin and Gerald Patterson (1975) found that mothers did not show any more positive responses to their children than fathers. Yet it is generally believed that fathers punish more and harder. Depending on the memory of high school students about their parental relations, Stinnett et al. (1974) found that the majority of both female and male students perceived the mother to be the greatest source of affection. It is difficult to know whether the high school student actually received more affection or whether their memory was influenced by the frequently accepted stereotype "Wait till Daddy comes home."

In nursery schools, teachers seem to treat boys and girls alike, but they reward feminine behaviors more often than masculine behaviors, though there is a difference between male and female teachers. In a nursery school caring for two-year-olds, Etaugh et al. (1975) observed that 83 per cent of the rewards of female teachers and 67 per cent of the rewards of male teachers were given for feminine behavior. Similar results were obtained by McCandless and Evans (1973) who counted how often the boys were rewarded by their female teachers for male and female sex-role activities. Of about 230 such observed rewards, 200 were for such "feminine" behavior as painting and art work and only 32 for such "masculine" tasks as block building and playing with transportation toys. With such frequent rewards for femininity, one should expect that the boys would engage more and more in feminine activities, but no such trend was noted during a year's observation period.

Are the efforts of the female teachers useless as far as three-year-old boys are concerned? If the teachers' rewards had any effect at all they were probably offset by the rewards given by peers. McCandless and Evans found also that boys reinforced other boys five times as often as they reinforced girls. An earlier study by Fagot and Patterson (1969) reported also that persons reinforce that behavior which is in their own repertoire. Peer influence seems to be especially strong in the modeling of toy preferences, curious and novel behavior, and aggressiveness; and adult influences seem to be strongest in verbal instructions about social rules and the correct solution of problems (Wolf, 1975).

Observers seem to agree about the type of stereotypy that exists in children's play behavior, but it does not seem to be clear whether girls or boys receive more cultural "pressures" to follow the accepted stereotypy; nor is it clear whether it is the father or the mother who exerts most of these cultural pressures. Several investigators (Fagot & Patterson, 1969; Etaugh et al., 1975) found that two-year-old boys select more toys from both sexes and Fagot (1974) observed that girls received more negative as well as more positive guidance than boys. This suggests that boys in their early childhood experience fewer restrictions and that girls are under more pressures to conform in this developmental stage. In observing families who had at least one male and one female child ranging from 5 to 12 years,

Margolin and Patterson (1975) found also that boys received more positive responses from their parents than did girls. While the boys are freer in their movements inside and outside the home they are more restricted with regard to sex-roles. A number of studies reviewed by Ruth Hartley (1967) and more recently by Seymour Fisher (1973) point to the conflicts boys are prone to have because they are required to conform more rigidly to the male sex-role. During later childhood it becomes more acceptable for girls to be tomboys than it is for boys to be sissies.

Even on such a variable as physical attractiveness (generally believed to be a criterion for judging females) boys are scrutinized and often discriminated against by their peers and also by women—their mothers and teachers. Unattractive preschool boys are rated as less popular and often as more antisocial than attractive boys (Karen Dion & Ellen Berscheid, 1974) and women behave more leniently toward an attractive boy than toward an attractive girl or an unattractive boy (Dion, 1974). It is difficult to know if the attractiveness criterion by which boys are judged becomes less important in adolescence and adulthood. There is no doubt that this criterion is a significant dimension for female adolescents and adults. Many beauty contests have survived in spite of strong opposition from female liberation groups. Although covert, the criterion of physical attractiveness may be as discriminatory for males as it is for females.

We obtain again many diverse data if we try to examine which parent plays the greater role in establishing sex stereotypes. In general the father seems to be the one who holds more definite opinions about sex stereotypes. Beverly Fagot (1973) observed toddlers and compiled a list of 38 different behaviors. She presented this list to mothers and fathers of two-year-olds asking them to rate the behaviors as to masculinity and femininity. She found that fathers were more certain in their ratings than mothers. Roughhouse play, for instance, was considered as masculine by all fathers, but not by all mothers; playing with dolls was considered feminine by almost all fathers, but by a much lower percentage of mothers. Fathers not being around as much are perhaps more likely to respond to cultural stereotypes, to what they think should be, while mothers may base their judgment on the actual behavior they observe.

It is questionable how much the father's attitude correlates with the actual interaction with his children. One of Fagot's later studies (1974) suggests that mothers punish more frequently than fathers and in Dion's study, mentioned above, it was found that women discriminated between attractive and unattractive children, while men did not. Fagot questioned married couples on the sex-appropriateness of certain toddler behaviors and found that the children of parents who checked many of the behaviors as appropriate to only one sex did not show any more sex typing in their behavior than the children whose parents checked almost all of the behaviors as equally appropriate for both sexes. More specifically, Fagot reports that there were three sets of parents who were such egalitarians that they were very upset at even being asked about sex differences, yet their children exhibited the same stereotyped toy preferences as the children of the parents who held very conventional views.

Data as the above suggest that the influence of parents with respect to toy preferences may be minimal and that their establishment may depend much on peers, television, and neighbors. We must further hypothesize that the cues that parents give are largely unknown to the parents so that they cannot alter them if they intend to teach nonstereotypy. Fagot (1974) presents an interaction view, mentioning that the child's behavior may exert pressures on the parent to behave differently to boys and girls. Girls, for instance, may receive more verbal praise and reproof than boys because they verbalize more than boys, thereby animating the parents to behave differently toward them in spite of the parents' good intentions to treat the sexes equally.

The research results about the parents' influence on sex-role stereotypy depend much on the socioeconomic status of the family observed as well as on the age, the number, and the sex of their children. The mechanisms and the modes by which sex-stereotypy can be established will be discussed in the following chapter.

School-age

There are hundreds of studies testing the sex differences of school-age children with regard to play activities, career choices, school success, anxiety, and attitudes toward self and others. At this age they may sit still long enough to be convenient study subjects.

Reviewing the type of games children play, Sutton-Smith and Sovasta (1972) found that boys from the ages between 5 and 12 preferred games involving strength, body contact, and a clear outcome of winning or losing. The games girls played during the same ages could be characterized by taking turns, choral activities, and verbalism.

With respect to games, it is interesting to compare the results of two studies that surveyed sex-role differences in chess playing. Eileen Price (1974) questioned 150 elementary school pupils in grades four, five, and six in Portland, Oregon. She found that about 25 per cent of the boys and 17 per cent of the girls reported that they could play chess. Gardiner (1974), who investigated the chess playing habits of 116 high school students in the same city, found that about 90 per cent of the boys and 60 per cent of the girls reported that they knew how to play. This shows that the total number of both boys and girls who learn how to play chess increases from grammar school to high school and that at each age level there are about one third more boys than girls who learn how to play. However, large differences were reported when the pupils were asked "How often do you play chess?" At the beginning at the elementary level, boys and girls played almost equally often, but at the high school level, 38 per cent of the boys but only 2 per cent of the girls fell into the "frequent" category (e. g., playing about 100 games per year). In the occasional category (e. g., playing about 10 games per year) there were twice as many boys as girls, and in the "now not playing at all" category there were 50 per cent of the girls and only 10 per cent of the boys.

It is difficult to say why the playing frequency of girls decreases so drastically. Do they give up because only 60 per cent of them know how to play as compared to the boys' 90 per cent, or has chess the image of a man's game? Although it is not specifically labeled a man's game, the news and the pictures of champion players present men almost exclusively, particularly in the more competitive stages. Several studies have shown that once a game is sex-typed it is not played as much nor as vigorously by the opposite sex. Montemayor (1974) presented children between six and eight with a neutral toy figure into which marbles could be inserted. He found that boys inserted more marbles into the toy when it was labeled as a toy for boys and that girls played more often with it when it was labeled a toy for girls. There were no sex differences when the toy was rated for attractiveness and the ratings, were congruent with the actual play behavior. Both sexes rated the toy with the sex-inappropriate label as less attractive.

Another study shows the influence of an actual person playing with a sex-inappropriate toy. Wolf (1973) had eight-year-old and nine-year-old boys watch another boy play with an oven with a kettle on it, a sex-inappropriate toy. Thereafter, the boy who was the model left the room and the boys who had watched him played readily with this sex inappropriate toy. Boys who had watched girls play with oven and kettle did not play with them after the girl model left and they were alone with these objects. "Same-sex" modeling was also effective for girls who saw another girl play with a truck and tire. Wolf's data support the environmental hypothesis; it was shown that under the right social condition, new toy behavior can be acquired. The appropriate social situation won out over the inappropriate toy!

School-age children have often been questioned about their attitudes toward vocations. It is known that four-year-old boys want to be policemen and four-year-old girls want to be nurses. (In the world of four-year-olds, one's safety and one's health is more than guaranteed!) As the children get older, their vocational choices become more diversified but still follow many sex stereotypes. Looft (1971) examined the vocational aspirations of first and second graders. The 33 boys questioned in his sample listed 18 different occupations. Football player, policeman, doctor, dentist, scientist, pilot, and astronaut were some of their most frequent choices. The 33 girls questioned responded with only eight different choices, with nurse and teacher being mentioned by 25 pupils.

Most obvious and most consequential for adult life are the sex-role differences related to the vocations. In almost all Western countries, women get paid 30 per cent less than men for doing the same—or often more unpleasant—work (see: Vocational Differences, Chapter 7). When elementary school children form their vocational preferences boys seem to model courage and daringness and girls seem to imitate helpfulness with respect to job characteristics. In high school characteristics of professionalism and expertness are added to the existing biases. Harriet Mischel (1974) investigated sex biases of professional achievements. Her subjects were high school and college students who were presented with professional articles in the areas of law, city planning, primary education, and dietetics. The same articles were presented to some students with the author's name as John R. Simpson and to others with Joan

R. Simpson. Both female and male students rated the professional achievement higher in law and city planning when the article was presented under the man's name and they rated it higher in dietetics when presented under the female name. The high school students were not too impressed by the female name in the primary education areas. Perhaps their own primary education experiences were too recent. Mischel replicated her experiment in Israel with both a city and a kibbutz sample. She found no sex biases as the articles were evaluated independent of the authors' sex. This again shows that these biases are culture bound.

Besides toy and games and vocational preferences, psychologists have examined attitudes and value systems toward self, others, objects, ideologies, etc. and have found sex differences in all of these areas. Rose Zelig (1962), for instance, investigated attitudes toward annoyances and irritations concerning health and appearance, hobbies and interests, foods, games and amusement. From questionnaires given to sixth graders, she composed a list of 37 items and found that 14 of these items showed significant sex differences. For instance, more girls than boys hate to have accidents, operations, headaches, and stomach aches. More girls hate to get hurt, be dirty, wear torn clothes, or drink milk. More boys hate to go to operas, take piano lessons, go to concerts, plant flowers, or eat carrots. Both boys and girls varied also in the degree to which they were irritated by certain situations in their daily lives. But who would have guessed the "milk - carrot" sex difference?

We may even question whether annoyances, irritations, or hates have the same meaning for boys as for girls. Ekehammar (1974) had 16-year-olds rate 18 different components of anxiety. Girls reported higher incidents in 12 out of these 18 components, such as "heart beats faster," "get feeling of panic," "stomach trouble," "hands shake," etc. As to which situations cause anxiety, girls responded also more frequently to such items as examinations, dentists, starting a new job, contests, alone in the woods, etc. In discussing these differential self-reports Ekehammar points out that males may have similar feelings but inhibit their reporting. He also discussed some physiological differences, such as higher female heart rates and differential amounts of adrenalin and no adrenalin secretions.

One way by which psychologists try to assess interpersonal relations is by measuring the distance people keep from each other during play, school, or professional activities. Lomranz et al. (1975) measured this "personal space" on preschool and school children in Tel-Aviv and found that less distance was kept from girls than from boys. There were no differences between boys and girls who did the approaching, but both sexes moved closer when the object of approach was female. Adults of both sexes show also a narrower personal space when approaching women than men. Lomranz et al. postulate that this behavior is learned and has generalized through the closeness to the mother, which both females and males experience in our culture.

College Students

Surpassed only by the white rat, the American college student has been studied and analyzed more than any other living being. A variety of opinions, attitudes, personalities, and behavior have been measured in many dimensions, often with emphasis on female and male differences. Even their dreams have been compared by Cohen (1973) who believes that the sex-role orientation is more basic to the dream content than the dreamer's biological gender. To what degree college students believe in the control of their own destiny has been assessed by McGinnies et al. (1974) who found that women in Australia, Japan, New Zealand, Sweden, and the United States believe to a greater degree than men that their lives are controlled by outside influences. The authors point out that the general philosophy of the Swedish college woman (as measured by the Internal-External Locus of Control Scale) was the same as in other countries, in spite of the fact that Sweden had equalizing and socialistic laws.

A large number of studies deal with the investigation of attitudes and personality variables related to vocational preferences. Hottes & Kahn (1974) observed certain character traits of pairs of females and pairs of males during a competitive game (Prisoners' Dilemma Game). They found that males are more success oriented and that their competitive behavior appears to be an attempt to maximize their gain. Women were more socially oriented and their choices of competitive responses appeared to be a defensive measure. Given the opportunity to communicate, females prefer to discuss nonstrategic matters and show less change in their game behavior.

Sex differences in the willingness of college students to help others were investigated by Bickman (1974). He had males and females ask others in various ways to volunteer for an experiment. When asked by telephone, 72 per cent of the males agreed to help female callers and 51 per cent agreed to help male callers. The female's preference for the opposite sex was not quite so strong; about 63 per cent agreed to help male callers and 52 per cent to help female callers. When the subjects were contacted for help by letter, 33 per cent of the males agreed to help when the letter was signed by a woman compared to 13 per cent when it was signed by a man. Of the females 53 per cent were willing to help when there was a man's signature and 22 per cent when there was a woman's signature.

The results of this experiment, and of many others discussed in subsequent chapters, show that sex-role attitudes and their influences on behavior are not a "yes or no matter." Not all men helped all women and not all men refused to help all men. The differences were a matter of degree and sex preferences (for those who were helped) or discriminations (for those who were not helped) and were made by both females and males. While the female showed a higher rate of volunteering, both sexes volunteered for the opposite sex about twice as often as they did for their own. Surprisingly, these opposite sex attractions disappeared when the asking was done face-to-face. Here 51 per cent of both male and female students agreed to volunteer no matter whether they were asked by a female or a male. One would think that if sex preferences do exist, they would be more pronounced in a visual than in a telephone or letter contact. It happens frequently in psychological experimentation that facts are revealed not predictable by our previous knowledge.

The character trait of "suggestibility" has traditionally been considered a female trait. The results of several experiments, however, suggest that men are just as susceptible to it or even more so. Sandra Bem (1975) examined how much college students conformed in a cartoon-rating situation when they had previously heard the ratings of others. She found that males and females were equally susceptible to the opinions of others. In another experiment Patricia Aletky and Albert Carlin (1975) attempted to investigate suggestibility by examining a placebo effect. They asked college students of both sexes to work on a pressure device with and without applying an inert jelly to the forearm, a jelly that was alleged to relieve muscular fatigue. They found that the males were much more influenced by the suggested effect.

College students were also used as subjects by Cookie Stephan (1974) in a simulated jury trial to assess sex prejudice in juries. The literature on juries in the United States suggests that many attorneys advocate the "opposites-attract" hypothesis. That is, they assume that men will favor female defendants and that women will favor male defendants. But the results of Stephan's test suggests the opposite. In her simulated murder trial, she found that males favored the male defendant and females favored the female defendant. Paternalism was not found to be a factor in her study. It may not be a factor in cases where females are accused of masculine crimes, such as murder or assault. Neither women nor men seem to change their same-sex preference whether judging alone or in groups. In actuality, however, juries of a single sex group are very rare, and it is still a matter of speculation whether the same-sex preferences are maintained in mixed-sex juries.

Many more psychological dimensions have been examined for sex differences. A large number of studies involve college students and their attitudes about educational preferences and the vocational choices of women. Some of these studies will be discussed in a following chapter on vocational differences.

DISCUSSION

Various sex-role stereotypes have been examined through developmental stages and certain constant factors have become apparent along developmental lines. Both parents show the same sex-role stereotypes in the child-rearing process, although the father has the stronger biases and plays the dominant role in reinforcing them. Toy preferences seem to be established by the age of three and remain fairly constant perhaps strongly influencing game and vocational preferences at grade-school age. Vocational preferences broaden with increasing age but remain for each sex within stereotyped lines. To the initial "policeman and fireman" preferences of boys are added doctors, pilots, and astronauts—adding status stereotypy to sex stereotypy.

The studies cited in this chapter have shown a certain dilemma with regard to the retraining or the unlearning of sex-roles. Fathers who spend less time with their children influence the establishment of sex-roles more than mothers and female teachers, who are around the child for many more hours. How can sex-roles be changed if those adults who are spending the most time with the child have the least influence? Another hindrance in changing sex-roles is the fact that females, although to a lesser degree, have the same cultural stereotypes as males. Both sexes judged males bigger and stronger than they actually were and both sexes rated articles on law as superior when presumably written by a man and articles on dietetics as superior when written by a woman.

Other studies suggest that retraining may be feasible and that the culturally established sex-roles may not be as ingrained as is generally believed. In Israel, for example, the evaluation of professional articles was not influenced by the author's sex. Neither were the college students in the United States influenced by the sex of the caller if the demand for volunteering for an experiment was made face-to-face. It was also shown that toy preferences can be changed by a different "sex-labeling" and by presenting a "sex-inappropriate" toy together with a "sex-appropriate" toy together with a "sex-appropriate" model.

Sufficient observations have been cited to show that sex-role stereotypy permeates many attitudes and behaviors at all ages. Yet the question how stereotypes are established and how they can be changed has not been answered. When we find that toy preferences do not exist at age one, but are present at age three it may appear that they arose spontaneously. When boys learn more from their absent fathers than from their teachers who are present, we may also get the idea that learning occurs spontaneously. Nothing, however, in the course of human development comes out of the clear, blue sky. Humans are born with urges and capacities, but the ways in which these urges and capacities find expression will depend on the learning environment. Thus, to examine the many possibilities in which sex-roles are transmitted from one generation to another, we must first examine the process of learning and modeling discussed in the following chapter.

Chapter 4

SEX-ROLE ACQUISITION–WAYS OF LEARNING

Sex-role stereotype becomes integrated into much of our personality, exhibiting itself in many of our thoughts and actions. From childhood we are taught what and what not to do and, in addition to these teachings, we model that which we see around us. Thus, our language and thoughts and much of our likes and dislikes, and, of course, our sex-role stereotypes become established through learning in one way or another. We have seen in the previous chapter that sex-roles are learned perhaps in a cumulative fashion during all phases of our development. We have also examined several studies that attempted to investigate whether they are primarily established through the mother, father, nursery teacher, or peers. While the sources and the times are important they do not tell us how the sex-roles are taught and learned; it is the purpose of this chapter to elaborate on the various ways by which humans learn.

Learning has been one of the central issues of psychology. A body of knowledge has been accumulated on the nature of rewards and punishment, on voluntary and involuntary training, and on the establishment of reflexes, habits, fear, emotions, and other likes and dislikes. Relatively little work has been done on the learning of the sex-roles themselves, because their definition and their origin are quite complicated and because the subject is relatively new to psychology. In spite of these circumstances it is hoped that a general discussion of the psychological principles of learning will give the reader an understanding of the many ways in which sex-roles can become established.

Conditioning

One of the simplest ways to demonstrate learning is by means of "classical conditioning." It is also called "Pavlovian conditioning" because Pavlov discovered, during a lifetime of experiments, many important relationships between stimuli and responses. Simple reflexes such as the sucking reflex can be conditioned soon after birth (Lipsitt, et al. 1967; Marquis, 1931). It is within the natural response repertoire of infants to make sucking motions when their lips are touched. We do not know why this occurs, but we know that they are born with this capacity. Through conditioning we can teach infants to make this sucking motion in response to any other stimulus that they can perceive: to a light, a bell, or to various stimuli to which sucking would normally not occur. For fastest conditioning, the new stimulus, the bell for example, should be rung 1/2 second before the already known stimulus, the touching of the lips. After several such pairings of bell and touch, the infant will begin to make sucking motions as soon as the bell is heard and the touching of the lips will no longer be necessary. In a strict sense, new responses cannot be taught. They must originally come from the organism itself, but they can be modified, lengthened or shortened, or made to occur to cues and in situations in which they did not occur previously.

Pavlov also discovered the phenomenon of "generalization," which will be discussed later in this chapter in relation to stereotypes and prejudice. Pavlov found that after organisms have been conditioned to salivate to a certain tone (e.g., the middle A on the piano) they will also salivate, although not so profusely, to other tones (e.g., middle C) that they have never heard before. Generalization occurs in all learning situations. If one wants to avoid it, one must use a discrimination procedure rewarding the response to one stimulus, but not to the other (to the middle A but not to the middle C).

Hundreds of conditioning experiments have been reported examining simple reflexes as well as more complex habits and emotions. The American behaviorists John B. Watson and Rosalie Rayner (1920) conducted one of the first experiments involving the conditioning of a child's emotion. They taught Albert, an 11-month-old boy, to fear a rat. While Albert played with the rat peacefully, they sounded a loud noise, which made Albert cry. After a few such associations of noise and rat, Albert began to cry when he saw the rat. Albert's fear of the loud noise transferred to the rat, which he previously had not feared. This type of classical conditioning is called "avoidance conditioning." It is sometimes successfully used for getting rid of undesirable habits, such as alcoholism, where the intake of alcohol causes severe nausea because a certain drug has previously been taken.

Classical conditioning can also be used to dispel fears and to transfer pleasures. This process called "desensitization" was first demonstrated by Mary Cover Jones (1924) with her two-year-old subject, Peter, who was afraid of rabbits. To make Peter unafraid, Jones gave him ice cream while she showed him a rabbit. This might have transferred Peter's dislike for the rabbit to the ice cream and may have made Peter fear both—the rabbit as well as the ice cream. To prevent this, Jones put the rabbit into a cage in a far corner of the room and on subsequent days brought the rabbit closer and closer until it was next to Peter. At no time during this "successive approximation" procedure did Peter show any fear or anxiety. Conditioning is generally successful if that which is liked is presented in full force, while that which is not liked is presented in small doses. Not only children, but adults are often conditioned by successive approximation. When we buy a car, it is shown to us in its full glory. Its price, however, the disagreeable part, is given to us in small doses: the down-payment, the monthly payments, the rate of interest, etc. Few people would buy a car if it was the other way around, if one had to pay the full price first and later received parts of the car bit by bit.

Reward and Punishment

Classical conditioning as well as other learning procedures depend greatly on reward and punishment. The loud noise was a punishment for Albert, which made him cry and taught him to avoid the rat. The ice cream was a reward for Peter; it taught him to like the rabbit. Even though there are a series of experiments (Wesley, 1971) indicating that learning can occur in the absence of reward and punishment, learning occurs more frequently and is more pronounced under reinforcing conditions. But few children are conditioned in experiments as were Albert and Peter, and few parents raise their children applying such distinct and "primary reinforcers" as food or pain. Most interaction with our children occurs through more subtle, or "secondary reinforcers," which in turn have been learned through their association with primary ones consisting of certain foods and certain visual, auditory, and tactile stimulations. There are individual differences as to the effect of primary reinforcers. Being held and cuddled pleases only about half of all infants, while it is quite annoying to almost 25 per cent of them (Schaffer & Emerson, 1964). Pain is a strong primary deterrent to most children, but it may be ineffective for those with high thresholds who are more insensitive and often hyperactive. As mentioned before, females are somewhat more sensitive to touch and perhaps also to auditory stimulation. It is, therefore, possible that such primary reinforcers as a slap or a loud and sudden voice are more effective conditioners for females than for males.

Since few parents offer food or give physical punishment to their children in connection with the establishment of sex-roles, we can assume that sex-role behavior and accompanying feelings are taught mainly through secondary reinforcers of either a verbal or nonverbal nature. The nonverbal secondary reinforcers can be facial gestures and bodily motions we make in response to a child's well-being or ill feelings in a more or less regular fashion. When a child eats well and experiences pleasure we are likely to smile, and these gestures will take on a rewarding effect. Conversely, when a child is hurt or feels pain we make grimaces and motions that will take on a punishing effect. Our person, in itself, may become very rewarding for the child to the degree we are present in situations where the child receives food or other comforts. Nonverbal cues may be important in the establishment of toy preferences, which children begin to show during their second year. A smile, a more prolonged look, or other interactions on the parent's part may suffice to reward playing with a certain toy. The rewards parents give their children may to a certain degree be determined by the children themselves. Girls are more verbal than boys and, as Fagot (1974) observed, they receive more verbal rewards and punishments than boys. Boys, who are less verbal, receive more nonverbal reinforcement by being more often joined by their parents during their play.

Words have a special significance in the course of human learning since they are our most frequent means of approval and disapproval. However, the reward or the punishment value as well as the meaning of each word must first be experienced through conditioning. By nature, words have no meaning whatsoever. A word will signal those objects, actions, or feelings that an organism perceived or experienced at the time the word was heard. The word "gift," for example, is mentioned to English-speaking children in connection with presents and pleasant situations and to German children in connection with poisons, danger, and unpleasantness. Thus, the same word will signal different meanings and evoke different feelings in different language groups because it was used in different circumstances. The word "good," for instance, can be used as a reward only to the degree it was used in situations in which the child experienced pleasure (e.g., eating, seeing, or feeling something pleasant). Conversely, the words "no" and "bad" can only be used as punishments or deterrents to the degree they were initially used in connection with pain or discomfort. Words sometimes lose their intended effect because they are used inconsistently. For example, when children eat cookies and experience pleasure, they may hear such words as "no" or "that is bad for you." These words, intended as deterrents, become associated with good feelings and pleasures. If such associative incongruencies occur too often, words such as "no" and "bad" may begin to mean "yes" and "good." No wonder there are credibility gaps between parent and child!

Instrumental Conditioning

In classical conditioning the wanted behavior was brought out (elicited) by a stimulus the experimenter purposely applied—with Albert, it was crying and fear brought out by a loud noise; with Peter, it was no crying and pleasure brought out by the ice cream. Although classical conditioning is very effective, it can only be used in situations in which we can bring out the wanted behavior at a specific time so we can pair it with a new stimulus (usually a word) that we have chosen. But for most of the behaviors and attitudes we wish to teach, we do not know any ready-made stimuli that would bring out the wanted behavior and we must first wait until the person performs (emits) the desired behavior and use a reward (or punishment) after it has occurred. This learning process is called "instrumental" or "operant" conditioning because it is the organism itself and not the experimenter or the parent who is instrumental or operates the occurrance of the wanted action.

There are many situations that require instrumental conditioning. Toilet training may serve as an example because there are no specific and external stimuli for defecation and urination and the parent must wait with approval until they have occurred at the appropriate place. The difference between classical and instrumental conditioning is only a matter of degree. Although there is no button to press to make a child urinate, the chances that a child will urinate can be greatly increased if we offer lots of liquids. But even after their consumption, it may still be 15 to 30 minutes until urination occurs—a time lag too long for most parents to stay with the child so they can guide him or her to the potty chair at the right time and to reward the child after urination has occurred at the appropriate place. Too often, toilet training is a lengthy and annoying process because for months the parent scolds the child for doing the wrong thing, urinating in the diaper, but rarely rewards him or her for doing it correctly because it requires some patience and ingenuity to see that the right response occurs at the right place (Wesley, 1971).

Most instrumental conditioning occurs in situations much less stressful than toilet training. It occurs with behaviors performed more readily in everyday situations. A child can touch a toy, look at the parents, smile, walk, and utter sounds. These behaviors are not brought out by the parents, but they are frequently rewarded, punished, or ignored, depending on the parents' own likings and on their ideas of appropriateness of a certain behavior. Parents give much of this differential reinforcement without being aware of it or without intending to do so. It has been postulated by Campbell (1968) that our habit of sleeping at night and being awake in the daytime may have been conditioned early in our infancy by the fact that parents pay more attention to the child's wakefulness at daytime, and they are much less rewarding toward it when it occurs at night.

Whether or not we are aware of it, we are modifying the behavior of children to a large extent by rewarding, punishing, or ignoring it after it has occurred. When children take their first step we may kneel on the floor, hold out our arms, smile, get a camera, etc.—a host of responses contingent upon the child's own action. When a child has a temper tantrum we may respond with groaning, spanking, shouting, ignoring, etc. Such actions, called rewards or punishments in classical conditioning, are designated with the more neutral term "contingencies" in instrumental conditioning procedures (Skinner, 1969, 1971). Our response is contingent upon the child's behavior, and it remains to be seen whether it will be called a reward or a punishment. Any contingency, a kiss or a spanking, will be considered a reward if it has increased a certain behavior —if, for example, it has caused more frequent tantrums. Conversely, any contingency will be called a punishment (a kiss or a spanking) if it has decreased the behavior to which it was applied. In Skinner's system a reward or a punishment is not defined by a preconceived notion but, in a rather individualistic manner, by the effect it has on a specific individual in a specific situation. The same contingency (shouting, for example) can increase the temper tantrums for one child but decrease them for another child. The essence of behavior modification is the search for contingencies that will change behaviors toward the desired direction. Because B. F. Skinner has investigated the effects of contingencies and the method of behavior modification for many decades, instrumental or operant conditioning is now called "Skinnerian" conditioning.

Much of instrumental conditioning is possible because behavior fluctuates by nature. Even the loudest child will be less loud and perhaps even quiet at times and different contingencies can be applied to these fluctuations—walking away to loudness, talking to the child during quiescence. We give many differential contingencies to our children during the development of their language. We are inclined to be silent when a child babbles a sound not fitting into our language, but should we hear a "ma" or a "da" we may smile, turn to the child, repeat the sound in the hope to hear a "mama" or a "dada."

Individual behavior fluctuations may form much of the basis by which we condition sex-role stereotypy. Though there are some gender differences there is also much similarity between the sexes, with both female and male infants fluctuating from noisy to quiet and from active to passive. These fluctuations are very susceptible to instrumental conditioning and especially to the application of differential contingencies. When a boy's behavior fluctuates toward activity, aggression, and exploration we may smile, look, talk, gesture, and interact; when it fluctuates toward being quiet, sitting still, or dependency, we may ignore it, frown, or walk away. With girls we may use similar contingencies applying them when their behavior fluctuates toward the opposite poles. We can assume that this differential conditioning continues along stereotyped precepts as the child gets older. Fathers are inclined to smile when their boys pick up a toy truck, but may show little reaction when their girls do the same. Conversely, they may smile when their girls play with a nursing set but show a different reaction when their boys do it. Mothers may react little when their sons come home dirty but much more so when their girls' clothes do not look neat. Several studies discussed in the previous chapters have shown that mothers and fathers support each other in the differential reinforcement they give to their girls and their boys, and Fagot's (1974) study suggests that the subtle and differential contingencies parents apply to sex-role behavior may be independent of their own attitudes toward sex-role stereotypy.

Moss's study (1967) mentioned in the previous chapter has shown that boy and girl infants do receive different contingencies at different times from the different sexes. Ban and Lewis's study (1974) also suggests that mothers react differently than fathers when touched by their one-year-olds and that fathers apply different contingencies when being looked at by their boys than when being looked at by their girls. We rarely know what these contingencies are because most studies investigated the children's and not the parents' behavior. A study by Margolin and Patterson (1975) specifically designed to analyze parental behavior showed that fathers gave twice as many positive responses to their sons as to their daughters, whereas mothers gave almost the same number of positive responses to boys and girls. Altogether the boys received more positive rewards than the girls since the parents did not differ in the total number of rewards they gave. A behavioral coding system was used in this study to register the parents' behavior that followed immediately antisocial or prosocial behavior of their children ranging in ages from 5 to 12. Positive parental behaviors included approval, attention, compliance, laugh, play, talk, and touch. Coded as negative were such parental behaviors as command negative, disapproval, humiliate, ignore, noncompliance, tease, and yell. The antisocial and prosocial behaviors of the children to which the parents responded were similarly defined. Although the results of this study do not tell us which specific sex-role behaviors were involved, they do give us a breakdown of the parental behaviors that fathers give to their sons and daughters in unequal amounts.

The effect of instrumental conditioning and behavior modification has been demonstrated by hundreds of studies (Bandura, 1969), but there are few investigations that apply specifically to the conditioning of sex-role stereotypy. In spite of this lack of direct empirical evidence it stands to reason that a good deal ot the sex differences in toy selection, attitudes, and self-concepts discussed in the previous chapter do not come about spontaneously but are taught knowingly or unknowingly by instrumental conditioning.

Modeling and Imitation

If we want to teach a child to say "thank you" we will have to say it a number of times, hoping the child will imitate or model his or her words after ours. Psychologists have different theories as to why humans imitate or model. Their disagreement centers around the necessity of reward. Some believe modeling is a natural drive occurring without a reward. Others think it occurs by a mere association of events and that a reward is not necessary. They point out that a person in a certain situation wants to experience or do that which was experienced before in a same or similar situation. Going to the beach, for instance, may entice us to swim, because we swam before at beaches or saw others do it. We want to do it by "association" even though the water may be cold and in no way rewarding. Still other theorists believe that a reward is necessary for modeling. They point out that we imitate a model without a reward because in the past we were frequently rewarded for all sorts of imitations so that now the mere act of imitation has taken on rewarding qualities. There are other hypotheses about human modeling. Bandura has reviewed them in detail in his book, *Psychological Modeling: Conflicting Theories* (1971). He has also shown experimentally that modeling can occur in the absence of reward.

Whatever the case, psychologists theorize and children model. Often we do reward our children with praise, smiles, and with many other contingencies when they imitate our language, eating behavior, cleaning habits, etc. We buy girls small brooms and dustpans, bathinettes and tea sets, and we buy boys trucks and cementmixers, all to facilitate modeling while maintaining our sex-role stereotypes. At times, however, modeling is not rewarded. Mothers sometimes touch and feel fabrics in department stores but slap their children for doing the same. The imitation of putting on lipstick or smoking may also fall on less fertile ground. The desire of younger siblings to model older ones is often so strong that they will try things beyond their capacity and will have to be inhibited in their imitation.

Television has become an important modeling object in our society. Bandura (1965) investigated the modeling of aggression and found distinct sex differences in the performance of aggression. In his experiment, 33 boys and 33 girls ranging in age from three to five watched a five-minute television program in which a model (a man) pushed, beat up, and scolded an adult-size, plastic "Bobo" doll. At the end of the film one third of the children (the model rewarded group) saw the model rewarded with candy, drinks, and praise for beating up Bobo. Another group (the model punished group) saw the model being scolded and spanked with a rolled-up newspaper for beating up Bobo. The last third served as a control group with the model's behavior having no consequences.

After the film the children were taken into a playroom containing a Bobo doll, balls, mallets, dart guns, as well as such other toys as farm animals and miniature furniture. The aggressive behavior of each child was observed and recorded for a ten-minute period. The group that saw the model rewarded and the group that saw the model's actions being without consequences showed an equal amount of aggression in the playroom. In both groups, boys attacked

Bobo on the average about 3.5 times in ten minutes and girls attacked it slightly less than 2 times. The group that saw the model punished imitated less and showed more pronounced sex differences, with the average number of attacks for boys being 2.5 and for girls almost zero. This first portion of Bandura's experiment has far-reaching sociological implications. It shows that boys imitate aggression whether or not the model's actions are rewarded, ignored, or punished. It shows further that girls, although to a lesser degree, also imitate aggression if the model is rewarded or ignored but not when the model is punished.

Bandura's experiment had a second part. After each child was observed in the playroom for ten minutes, an experimenter entered offering each child fruit juice, toys, booklets, stickers, etc. for attacking Bobo. Under these new "imitator-reward" conditions, the boys of all groups increased their attacks to about four times and the girls of all groups to about three times, to almost as much as the boys. The girls, in other words, did not imitate aggression on their own initiative if they saw the model punished but did so if a reward was offered to them directly for performing the aggressive act. In this connection Bandura points out that there is a difference between learning and performing, that the girls who saw the model punished learned to imitate aggression while viewing the film, but did not perform until rewarded. In general his results suggest that girls are capable of learning and of performing aggression but are culturally in a precarious balance between the ages from three to five with respect to this trait. Seeing the model rewarded diminishes much of their previously learned inhibition and so they imitate. Seeing the model punished reinforces their previously learned inhibition and they do not imitate. Being themselves rewarded counterbalances this inhibition and they imitate again.

The model was a male in Bandura's experiment, and it is possible that the boys imitated more aggression than the girls because they were exposed to a male model. Wolf's experiment (1973) discussed in the previous chapter did show strong same-sex modeling in toy playing and the same must be postulated if we interpret the results of Sarah Sternglanz and Lisa Serbin (1974) who examined the ten most popular commercially produced children's television programs and found that half these programs did not portray any female roles. Of their total viewing time boys and girls watch men about 75 per cent of the time and women 25 per cent. One must postulate same-sex modeling, otherwise girls would become more masculine than feminine if the mere time and frequency of viewing were the dominant factors.

Same-sex modeling is not the only variable that influences modeling. The trait or the behavior to be modeled may be of equal importance. When Fryrear and Thelen (1969) examined the modeling of affectionate behavior toward a clown doll, they found that girls imitated both male and female models more often than boys. They also found same-sex modeling since the girls imitated female models more often that male models. The boys who imitated less imitated female and male models to an equal degree.

Same-sex modeling was also found in an experiment by Stephen Portuges and Norma Feshbach (1972) who investigated the imitation of incidental words and gestures. In their experiment eight- to ten-year-old pupils watched two four-minute films showing two female teachers giving geography lessons with additional "incidental" behavior. One teacher used such incidental remarks as "think hard" and "think carefully" and such incidental gestures as pointing to her forehead and clasping her hands. The other teacher said often, "listen carefully" and "you are not listening," and cupped her ear and folded her arms frequently. After seeing these two model teachers on film the pupils were asked to give a geography lesson to two life-size dolls. The pupils were observed for their imitative behavior, and it was found that the female models were imitated by the girls two to four times more often than by the boys. When examined for their social class it was further found that "advantaged" girls imitated most often, "advantaged" boys second most, "disadvantaged" girls third, and "disadvantaged" boys fourth.

The above experiment showed that much of the incidental behavior—specific words and gestures not related to the geography lessons—was transmitted through modeling, and quite effectively so, considering that the film strip lasted only four minutes. This suggests further that parents and teachers may teach their youngsters at any one time more than they intend to teach. They may transmit pat phrases, gestures, mannerisms, and attitudes of which they may or may not be aware. Neither may the learners be aware of what they have learned or are learning. While the pupils think they are learning geography, they are also learning to say "think hard" or to point their finger to the forehead. This double uncertainty of not knowing exactly what is taught and of not knowing exactly what is learned is one of the great stumbling blocks to changing the culture through a teaching-learning process.

The uncertainty about what or whom we imitate is again brought out in a study by Havelick and Vane (1974). Their models were black and white female teachers and their observers were black and white pupils. The task in their experiment consisted of marking the one of three lights that was expected to go on. In addition to this imitation task, the pupils were also asked to rate the competency of their teachers. It was found that the black pupils rated the black model as far more competent than the white model. But in spite of this rating, the black pupils imitated the white teacher more often than the black teacher. Our uncertainty about learning can even turn into a contradiction between what is intended to be learned and what is actually learned. This contradiction may only be an apparent one if we realize that imitation and judgments depend on previous learning. The black pupil had learned previously in specific situations to rate blacks as superior and in other specific situations to imitate white teachers. Although the situations were combined, the separately learned behaviors were maintained.

An increasing number of experiments on modeling and imitating are reported from year to year in the psychological literature. Havelick and Vane (1974) have reviewed a number of imitation studies and list the following characteristics as contributing to a model's success: prestige, warmth, aggressiveness, competence, power, dominance, and experience. These traits elicit more imitation than a display of their opposites. Traits of the imitator that further modeling have been found to be: dependency, cooperation, competitiveness, self-esteem, emotional disturbance, prior history of success and failure, and socioeconomic and racial stature. Who can fail to model with such a variety of prerequisites to choose from?

Generalization and Stereotypes

Sex-roles or sex-stereotypes are often considered as prejudism by those for whom they have disadvantages and as preference by those for whom they have advantages. Prejudisms and stereotypes are learned, and in order to understand and counteract them it will be useful to examine the processes by which they are learned.

Stereotyping can be considered a natural by-product of learning. Psychologists, however, refer to it as "generalization," a much less emotional term. It was previously described how Watson and Rayner conditioned the infant Albert to fear a rat. After this conditioning experiment, Albert was shown a rabbit, a white Santa Claus mask, and a piece of cotton. To all of these, he responded with crying. How could Albert be afraid of a rabbit? He was 11 months old, raised in a hospital and had never seen a rabbit before in his life. Psychologists really do not know why this happens, but they do know that similar objects, animals, and people will bring out similar reactions. They call such occurrences "generalization." It is quite natural for a child who was bitten by a dog to fear some other dogs or perhaps all other dogs, including those that do not bite. If the child is now running away from a friendly dog instead of feeding it, then this generalization is just plain prejudice from the dog's point of view. What can be done if a child has generalized the fear to all dogs? Such a general fear may become quite a nuisance to the child later on and the parents may want to counteract it. This means that they will have to teach their child that only certain dogs bite and that certain others do not. Such a process is called "discrimination." In comparison to generalization it is a much more cumbersome process; it requires finer distinctions in the learning process and better developed and better trained sensory organs. A single discrimination (e.g., whether or not to touch a dog) may require a number of finer distinctions. In our example a parent may show a dog to the child, pointing out such nonbiting cues as licking, pawing, and tail wagging and such biting cues as barking, growling, gnashing, and a rigid stance. One must, however, be careful showing the negative cues since they may again remind the child of the original fearful incident.

In some cases it is very difficult to counteract generalization because the child who has been bitten will stay away from all dogs; it is then impossible to introduce nonbiting dogs and teach the nonbiting cues. As mentioned before, Mary Cover Jones (1924) was successful in reconditioning Peter not to fear rabbits, but she took time and precautions by introducing the rabbit little by little and only at times when Peter was eating ice cream. Generalization develops rather suddenly and need not be taught, while discrimination on the other hand is a slower process and often needs the active help of a parent or teacher.

It should be noted that the psychological term "discrimination" describes the perception of smaller stimulus units. In the vernacular "discrimination" has all sorts of meanings. It connotes something good when we say a "discriminating taste," but something bad if just plain "discrimination." When an employer discriminates against women he is, psychologically speaking, *not* discriminating, but generalizing. According to his own preconceived notions, he believes that all women are unsuitable for the job and he is *not* willing to discriminate between those who may or may not be suitable.

Generalization does not only occur in the learning of fears or unpleasantness. It occurs also during the acquisition of our pleasures, trust, confidence, etc. People who love horses will generally like ponies, donkeys, barns, and saddles. If we have been pleasantly stimulated by a certain person, we will feel comfortable with a person of a similar type, although discrimination may get the better of us later! Both generalization and discrimination are very necessary for the learning process, but how much we should generalize and discriminate within and between the sexes is still much of an open question.

We need not always link prejudice and stereotypes to good or bad experiences. They may also arise through mere absence of nonacquaintance. If a child eats or sees no sardines or a similar food for the first ten years of his or her life, one can be quite certain that sardines will be disliked, even hated. We may say that the mere nonacquaintance or the not eating of sardines has become a habit, and organisms are by nature reluctant to change habits. It would perhaps take a slow conditioning process to make our ten-year-old like sardines. They may have to be paired with favorite foods and offered when the learner is hungry. The reader may think of his or her most disliked food and of the steps it would require to make this food likable.

A change in habits is usually more disturbing when one part of a familiar object remains the same and when another part changes. If young children, for example, have always seen their father with a beard it would be quite disturbing to them if he suddenly came home without it. It would be equally disturbing if the children had never seen their father with a beard and he returned unexpectedly with it from a war or a masquerade shop. In both cases there is, as psychologists would say, a "perceptual dissonance." Something familiar has been put together with something unfamiliar. This is often much more upsetting than seeing two unfamiliar things. The children in our examples would have been much less disturbed seeing a stranger with a beard.

Prejudism may often be based on a perceptual dissonance. Older people in our society were conditioned to such male characteristics as low voices, body types, and short hair for a very long time. All these stimuli have become very familiar to them. Now if some of these very familiar aspects are paired with just one unfamiliar one, long hair, a perceptual dissonance or a personal disturbance should be expected.

There may be several reasons why it is so difficult to overcome a perceptual dissonance. First we may feel our discomfort but may be unable to understand it logically. One may reason that a man with long hair should not be upsetting, but such reasoning may not remove the dissonance and the uncertainty it causes. At times of uncertainty, people are likely to hang on to myths, and those who feel uncomfortable seeing a man with long hair will feel more comfortable telling themselves and their neighbors that men with long hair are also lazy, dirty, untrustworthy, etc. There may be a second reason why it is so difficult to overcome a perceptual dissonance. Once we experience it, we are likely to stay away from it. Short-haired men are likely to stay away from long-haired men, which diminishes their chances of becoming familiar with the unfamiliar part of the dissonance. The long-hair issue was of particular difficulty in our society. Long hair was not only an unfamiliar male cue, but a familiar female cue, thereby causing perhaps a double dissonance for some and an obstinate prejudice for others.

Examining prejudice from the standpoint of learning, it becomes apparent that it is a rather natural phenomenon and that the one who holds the prejudice may be as uncomfortable with it as the one toward whom it is directed. This is not to say that those who suffer from prejudice should not try to counteract it. From the learning and retraining methods we have examined in this chapter, it would seem that conditioning by successive approximation would be one of the surest ways to counteract prejudice and stereotyped attitudes and behavior.

DISCUSSION

Classical conditioning, instrumental conditioning, and modeling may only be convenient categories to describe different ways in which learning occurs. The basic learning process or that which happens in the brain during learning is not known, mainly because the brain contains billions of individual nerve cells and interconnections. Their functions with respect to learning, thinking, and memory are still unexplored. In spite of our incomplete knowledge about the neurology of learning, psychologists have described and can predict much of our learning by having observed stimulus and response relationships.

Experiments have been discussed that show that fears, pleasures, the meaning of words, attitudes, and interests can be established through learning. Hundreds of additional experiments could be cited to demonstrate that the classical and instrumental conditioning processes permeate our entire lives, setting directions for most of our likes and dislikes. They include many of our preferences for foods, people, and objects and our intellectual inclinations. However, there are few classical or instrumental conditioning experiments that have directly investigated the establishment of sex-role stereotypy and many examples given in this chapter are based on analogous reasoning and not on empirical evidence. The data presented on modeling had a more empirical base. They showed that a number of factors determine whether and to what degree modeling will occur. These factors include the sex of the model, the nature of reward, the type of behavior to be modeled, and the sex and the social status of the viewer.

In spite of all these hindrances, certain general relationships have been demonstrated that are useful to understand learning situations including the training and retraining of sex-roles. Within limits it can be predicted that certain rewards will increase the occurrence of certain behaviors and that certain punishments will decrease them. We can verify and correct our results by examining the effects of contingencies. We can also be certain that generalizations, prejudism, and stereotypes occur first in the learning process and that their elimination is also a matter of learning, which takes longer and may need the active help of a teacher. A child will first call all men "daddy," including the milkman, and will only learn later to distinguish who is who. It has also been shown that any new habit or behavior that is not readily accepted is best introduced by successive approximation. These and other general principles discussed in this chapter should help those parents and teachers who have more-or-less definite plans on how much or how little "feminine" and "masculine" behaviors they would like to teach their offspring.

Chapter 5

INTELLECT AND EDUCATION

Although individuals are taught in the same manner, they learn at different speeds and remember different amounts for different lengths of time. In the search for the causes of these differences psychologists have examined such intellectual functions as intelligence, attitudes, creativity, and modes of thinking. Their hope is to find out which human tasks depend on which intellectual functions and to what extent these human functions depend on heredity or environment. In this chapter we shall examine and compare the intellectual capacities of females and males and the differential rates of their intellectual development. We shall also examine certain parental and educational practices that contribute to or reflect these differences.

Intelligence

In spite of the many controversies concerning the origins of intelligence, tests such as the Stanford Binet (1960) and the Wechsler-Bellevue (1953) assess a number of intellectual functions, including verbal facility, memory, numerical ability, and spatial relations, all of which are parts of the concept of "general intelligence." Men and women are equal in this general intelligence since there is no difference between their average scores. However, some sex differences become apparent when we compare male and female performance on some of the components that make up general intelligence.

Hannah Book (1932) gave 475 men and 475 women a battery of four subtests of the IQ and found that men were superior in maze problems and block counting, whereas women were superior in a cross-out pattern test and in a number-checking test. In a chapter on sex differences in her book, *The Psychology of Human Differences* (1965), Leona Tyler examines many studies and summarizes that males are clearly superior on tests of mathematical reasoning, spatial relationships, and science. Females are superior in verbal fluency, rote memory, perceptual speed, and finger and hand dexterity.

Not only do psychological tests indicate male-female differences in these intellectual functions but they also become apparent when their actual school performance is compared. In a "National Assessment of Educational Progress" study by Judith Sauls and Robert Larson (1975) which involved almost one million students throughout the United States, it was found that the sexes' performances are equal in science, mathematics, social studies, and citizenship up to the age of nine. By the age of 13, however, girls begin to fall behind in these areas and remain behind in their adult years. On the other hand, girls are ahead until the age of 17 in reading ability and in their literary knowledge. This survey reported an overwhelming lead of boys in geometry but few differences in arithmetic.

There seems to be no question that sex differences in these various intellectual abilities exist, but it should be reemphasized that it is not known whether or to what degree they are of innate or of cultural origin. One may also wonder why so much attention is given to these differences since the male and female "superiorities" are very slight, representing perhaps only a few IQ points (plus or minus) on the various subtests and that they represent averages with much overlap between the sexes. But, as has been pointed out before, small and seemingly unimportant differences may lead to more important ones if they are reinforced by others or by the individual's own behavior. If boys, for instance, are slightly better in manipulating and thinking about space orientation they may find it more suitable to play with building blocks, trucks, and mechanical objects. Such continued manipulations may "fortuitously" (without parental action) reinforce mechanical curiosity and aptitude.

Girls being verbally inclined may find it more satisfying to play with dolls to which they can talk and to play at tea parties where they can talk and sing. While they engage in these activities their mechanical and spatial abilities may become neglected. There may be a similar reason why girls advancing from grammar-school age to high-school age play less and less chess since chess playing depends more on spatial than on verbal abilities. The small differences between female and male capacities can become decisive motivational factors during the educational process.

Liking words just a bit more than arithmetic may conduce a girl to do better homework in English during her grammar-school years, to take history rather than physics as an elective in high school, to take a nonscience major in college, and consequently to become an English teacher and not a dentist. A small initial preference becomes more and more binding by the time certain intermediate or final educational steps are reached. Many writers who advocate sex equality ask that boys and girls be given equal educational chances to explore their own talents. However, just the contrary, a fixed curriculum that prescribes for both sexes science as well as nonscience subjects, may best serve educational equality. Choice seems to allow the influence of hereditary preferences as well as the influence of already existing stereotypes.

Intellectual Growth

Throughout life, females are slightly more verbal than males. Manifestations of this difference begin on the second and third days of life. When Korner (1969) observed various behaviors of newly-born infants he found that boys consistently showed startled behavior while girls engaged more frequently in reflex smiles and bursts of rhythmic mouthing. Moss (1967) found that by the age of three months females babble and vocalize more than males. It is also interesting to note that those female infants who babble much during the first and second years of their lives will have larger vocabularies at the ages of three and four and higher IQ's in adult life than those girl infants who babble little during early infancy. Several studies (McCall & Kagan, 1967; Cameron et al., 1967; Moore, 1967) have shown that this correlation exists in girls, but not in boys. This means that the amount of babbling in boys does not predict the size of their vocabulary nor their IQ's in later years.

Theories have been advanced to explain why babbling is predictive for girls and not for boys. Acheson (1966) maintains that girls develop faster and are developmentally older than boys so that their behavior at the age of one and two is more regular and hence more predictive. Sutton-Smith (1973) suggests a differentially acting neural system for girls who respond with babbling when stimulated acoustically or visually. Moss (1967) believes that the girls who babble more frequently are more consistently rewarded by their mothers and that this consistency is responsible for the predictability. He observed that well-educated mothers verbalized more with their girl infants than those who were less well-educated. He found no such difference in the mother-boy relationships.

In early childhood girls engage in more verbal play activities. In the first grades they are better readers and have superior word recognition. Samuels and Turnure (1974) found that superiority in word recognition was related to better attentiveness. By the age of ten, boys seem to have caught up with girls, but divergence occurs again about age eleven. Maccoby and Jacklin (1974) point out that female superiority increases through high school and possibly beyond. More specifically, girls are superior on such tasks as understanding and producing language, verbal analogies, creative writing, word fluency, and spelling.

The verbal superiority of females seems to be innate at least in its initial phase. The same assumption cannot be made for the numerical and spatial ability of males, because their onset does not become apparent until the early school years with years of opportunities for cultural influences. Males retain the lead in spatial and numerical ability through high school and college, although women do better in computations and counting. In spite of the fact that males are superior in numerical, spatial, and arithmetical abilities, females receive better grades in grammar school for these subjects. This may sound like a contradiction, but it should be explained that our intellect can be measured by achievement tests measuring that which has been learned (e.g., how many Spanish words one knows) and also by capacity or intelligence tests measuring the speed and the thoroughness by which individuals learn (e.g., how fast and how well one can learn Spanish words). Grades in grammar school seem to reflect achievement more than capacity as they depend more on the amount of work and on cooperation with the teacher (Walberg, 1969).

Ursula Lehr (1972) has reviewed the literature on the mathematical capacity more specifically and reports that girls in preschool have a better understanding of numbers and that between the ages of 6 and 14 they are almost equal to boys in arithmetical calculation. This, however, does not include problems involving geometrical understanding nor the type of arithmetical problems derived from a verbal description, the so-called "story problems." This difficulty was again reported by Sauls and Larson (1975) in their National Assessment Study where girls were found poorest in the applied arithmetical problems, such as figuring the lowest per-ounce price for a box of rice. These findings are somewhat surprising as the applied or story problems involve verbal skills in which girls excel and also arithmetical skills in which girls equal boys. It is puzzling why girls perform poorly when these two skills are combined, be it that an applied problem requires not only a verbal input and an arithmetic output, but a "geometric" or as yet undefined capacity to transform the given words into an arithmetical problem. A pupil, for instance, may have to visualize the package of rice and imagine some geometric partitions of the unit components before writing down the actual arithmetic problem.

Despite the difficulty psychologists have in defining mental components, the memorization capacity has been fairly well categorized. It includes tasks requiring the exact repetition of words, numbers, stories, and reproduction of geometrical figures; and it has been found that females excel in these tasks. It is interesting to note that females excel in the memorization of geometrical figures but not in geometry itself. May and Hutt (1974) tested the ability of nine-year-old boys and girls to recall and to recognize two-syllable nouns. Recall is a memory task without aide (e.g., "What was this word?") while recognition tests provide cues like the alternatives on a multiple choice test (e.g., "Was the word table, sofa, or window?"). Girls scored higher than boys on both recall and recognition tasks. In adult years some of the memory differences seem to level off. Epstein (1974) found no sex differences in recall at the college level and Nancy Bayley (1970) presents a graph showing that females perform equal to males in digit memory by the age of 30.

What are some of the magnitudes of the reported sex differences? What does it mean when we say better, superior, slightly superior, etc? A partial answer may be obtained from the study by May and Hutt mentioned above. Looking closer at the results, we find that boys could recall 7.3 and girls 7.6 nouns from an original list of 20. These were the scores of the nine-year-olds who had the words presented to them visually by slides and there were practically no sex differences. A larger difference was obtained when the words were presented auditorily by tape with the boys recalling 4 and the girls 7 out of 20 correctly. One or several factors could be responsible for the boys' poorer memory on the auditory part of the experiment: The material was verbal, the task was memory, and the voice on the type was female—factors that are in general more negative for boys than for girls.

Cognition

It has become fashionable in psychology to call the thought process (or processes) by which a problem in analyzed and solved the "cognitive style." How many cognitive styles are there and do the sexes use different cognitive styles or different mental approaches when they solve the same problem? There are no definite answers to these questions. Even the thought processes involved in the simplest problems have eluded psychological investigation. Do the multiplication problems, 3×10, 3×11, and 3×17, for instance, require the same type and amount of "thinking" for their solution? Does one problem require verbal memory, the other a visual imagery, and the third a combination of these two or some other process? Is there any difference between knowledge and understanding, or is understanding just additional knowledge?

Psychologists simply do not know what goes on in a person's brain during problem solving. The function of the mind is usually described by its product—the right or wrong outcome of a problem—hence the psychologist's judgment about the cognitive style of the sexes will depend on the problem on which the comparison is based. Eleanor Maccoby and Carol Jacklin (1974), who reviewed over 2,000 articles and books on sex differences, state that the sexes do not differ on tests of cognitive style that measure the ability to analyze problems. However, Nash (1970) in his psychobiological approach to developmental psychology, lists a series of experiments that suggest that the sexes do use different approaches in certain instances. Boys, for instance, were found to be able to transfer knowledge more readily from one problem to another, not only in the science part, but also in the home economics part of a certain test (Kostich, 1954). Also males were found to solve a "horse-trading" problem more often than females, and females in mixed groups solve it more often than in all-female groups (Hoffman and Maier, 1961).

At times it is not only the nature of a problem, but also the condition under which the solution is to occur that will effect sex differences. For example, when a time limit was imposed on a discussion task, it increased male efficiency, but decreased female efficiency (South, 1927). A series of experiments in perception have shown that females tend to be more influenced by their perceptual surrounding. Judging a vertical line within a tilted frame, females are more influenced by the tilted frame. Their "cognitive style" in this situation has been defined as "field-dependent," in relation to males who are said to be more "field-independent" (Witkin et al., 1954, 1962).

Broverman et al, (1968) present a biochemical view and suggest that male hormones (androgen steroids) affect the neural function in a relaxing and inhibitory (cholinergic or trophotropic) way. This may enable the male to react more slowly and to consider previous experience, a mode of response useful for novel situations. This views the female nervous system as more wakeful and faster reacting (adrenergic or ergotropic) and better adapted to perceptual and motor tasks that require fast reactions.

It is perhaps too early to set up hypotheses pertaining to cognitive styles when there are still many unknowns about cognitive processes. Several experiments investigating the concept of "horizontality" may serve as an example to show that a slight change in experimental procedures results in different responses from males and females. The horizontality concept first tested by Piaget and Inhelder (1967) pertains to the principle that the surface of still water remains horizontal, independent of the position of its container. In order to test this concept subjects are shown a bottle in an upright position, half-filled with red-colored water. They are then shown a similar, empty bottle in a tilted position—for instance, 45°—and are asked to indicate where the water level would be if this tilted bottle was half-filled.

It has been shown by Essex et al. (1971) and also by Wesley (1971) that by the age of eight, about 75 per cent of the boys and girls know this principle of horizontality and 95 per cent of the boys and girls can master this concept after some practice. Munsinger (1974) repeated these experiments with female college students and reported also about 90 per cent correct answers. In all the above experiments, the water level had to be drawn or to be indicated by marking the correct alternative in a multiple choice test.

Quite different results were obtained by Thomas et al. (1973) who tested university freshmen and reported in *Science* magazine that half their female subjects did not know the concept of horizontality and had difficulty learning it. Thomas et al., however, asked their subjects to indicate the correct water level by rotating a cardboard behind another piece of cardboard that had an opening in the form of a tilted bottle. It is plausible to assume that this somewhat apparatuslike model caused 50 per cent of the females to respond incorrectly. What was believed to be an inadequacy in understanding the horizontality concept may have been caused by an unfamiliarity to deal with the apparatus in this experimental situation. We should emphasize again that a slight change in the problem or in the required response or in the circumstances in which it is presented may cause age-specific and sex-specific differences as was also shown on the memory task where the performance of boys diminished when the material was presented by sound rather than by vision.

Motivational and other personality variables further confound the definition of cognitive style. Walberg (1969) studied over 2,000 girls and boys collecting 58 different cognitive, attitudinal, and behavioral measures. He found girls to score higher on verbal, social, cautiousness, and aesthetics; boys scored higher in autonomy, preference for mental manipulations rather than people, dogmatism, and rejecting conformity. He also found that the traits in which the girls excelled were conducive to better school grades while the traits in which the boys excelled correlated with those of successful scientists.

Creativity is another intellectual function difficult to define and even more difficult to measure. Some consider it to be one of the cognitive styles and others believe it is a mental function of its own. Its categorization is difficult because some people are "all-around" creative, others only in certain areas. Was Van Gogh more creative than Picasso, Faulkner more creative than Fulton? These questions cannot be answered, although no one doubts that all four were creative. Perhaps everybody is creative in his thoughts, but we notice it only in those people who have opportunities, chance, and a good press agent. In spite of these fundamental difficulties, psychologists have managed to design several tests for creativity. These tests usually measure flexibility by asking for various ways to solve a problem (e.g., "In how many different ways can one use a brick?"). Independence, sensitivity, and perceptual openness have also been used as measures of creativity. Ursula Lehr (1972) reviewed the literature on creativity and found that some toy tests indicate that boys are more creative in early childhood because they accept new toys more readily, but that girls are equal and even more creative in later childhood, especially in story telling and creative writing. She concludes, however, that there are no clear differential sex traits.

Creative men have often been judged more feminine and creative women more masculine than their respective norms. From this, Torrance (1962) hypothesizes that creativity requires sensitivity as well as independence, feminine as well as masculine traits. Nash (1970) cites McKinnon who believes that highly creative people have developed a nonstereotyped life style having refuted or having changed the given sex-roles.

Parental Settings

How much does the environment influence the intellect? What can parents contribute to their children's intellect, intelligence, school grades, and more specifically to their children's verbal and mathematical abilities? These questions have occupied psychologists for decades and those who evaluate the success of such compensatory educational programs as Head Start, Latch Key, and day care programs. Jensen (1969) in his controversial article "How much can we boost IQ and scholastic achievement?" cited several data from the U.S. Civil Rights Report indicating that the compensatory or enrichment programs did not have the beneficial effect on IQ and scholastic achievement as was originally assumed.

Even if a major portion of the IQ is genetically determined and a minor portion environmentally determined,
there is still enough leeway in the environmental portion to
equalize most of the existing differences. For example, the
IQ of black children from the Southern United States increases an average of seven points after they have lived in
the North for several years. On the other hand, one will
rarely be successful in raising a child's IQ more than 15 or
20 points, but an increase from 5 to 10 points can frequently be accomplished. This increase would easily take
care of any sex differences linked to verbal and mathematical abilities.

Although we know that IQ and intellectual functions
are influenced and changed by environment, we hardly
know which environmental factors are responsible for such
changes. What should a parent do to further a certain intellectual capacity in the child? Within the limits of change,
mothers and fathers have a different influence on their boys
and a different influence on their girls. In one of the most
thoroughly conducted longitudinal studies, the Berkeley
Growth Study, Nancy Bayley and her associates observed
and collected data on infants and their mothers and fathers.
They tested their subjects periodically until the children
were 40 years old. The Berkeley Growth Study has yielded
a wealth of data including those of Bayley and Schaefer
(1964), who examined maternal behavior until the children
were 3 years old and correlated it with the children's IQ
taken during the ages from 7 to 18. They found that boys
who are treated positively and nonauthoritarian by their
mothers during the ages 0 to 3, will tend to have a higher
IQ during later childhood and adolescence. As may be
expected, all forms of "negative" maternal treatment—
anxiety, irritability, perceiving the child as a burden, punitiveness, and ignoring—have a lowering effect on later IQ.

Unexpectedly, none of the above mentioned maternal
behaviors, neither the "positive" nor the "negative" ones,

had any affect on the future IQ of the daughters. Bayley (1968) believes that there is a genetic difference between the sexes. Boys are more susceptible to environmental conditions and as she states "more permanently effected by the emotional climate in infancy whether it was one of warmth and understanding or of punitive rejections." Girls are apparently less influenced by their environment and in Bayley's words, "more resilient in returning to their own characteristic inherent response tendencies." There was one maternal trait, "concern about health," which influenced the girls' IQ negatively, but the boys' IQ positively. Bayley and Schaefer's results agree with other studies that have found girls to develop physiologically and pscyhologically more evenly and more predictably than boys.

What about the effect of the father? Marjorie Honzik (1967), who also used data from the Berkeley Growth Study, reports that the opposite parent has a stronger effect. The mother-son relationship appears to be crucial for the boys' behavior between the ages from 8 to 18. For the girls, on the other hand, a "friendly" relationship with the father is more important for their performance between 5 and 17. Comparing the same sexes, Honzik found that the fathers' occupational success and satisfaction influences the boys' IQ and that the mothers' educational level influences the girls' IQ. Reppucci (1971) reported that a father at home contributes to the "masculine" mind and to a higher IQ for both boys and girls, but Rees and Palmer (1970) reported that boys from broken homes gain less on IQ than boys from intact homes. This differential home situation had no effect on the girls' IQ, supporting again the results of Bayley that girls are more resilient toward environmental influences.

In practice, there is not much that can be done to change children's IQ's. The correlations between any particular family setting and the IQ are low, meaning that the family setting, whatever it is, does not greatly influence the IQ. Anyway, few persons are likely to take mates just to increase their children's IQ a few points! Another limiting factor is the IQ's "threshold effect." Enrichment will be of little effect after a certain level has been reached. This can be compared with a child's growth and food intake; food denied below a certain amount would stunt a child's height, but food offered above this amount would not increase it. It has also been reported (Jensen, 1969) that a child's IQ is not so important for success in grammar school as are factors in the child's home environment such as the socioeconomic level and the parental interest in school and homework. This relationship is reversed on the high-school level, where the IQ correlates higher with success than with conditions at home.

Education

The educational system has received much criticism for propagating sex-role differences. Parts of its personnel, budget, curriculum, and instructional material are heavily male oriented. Obvious examples are the male-dominated administration and the importance of football, which receives an aproportional amount of the budget, often more than all the "women" sports combined. Leonore Weitzman et al. (1971) have made a content analysis of the Caldecott Award–winning children's books published between the late 1960s and early 1970s. In 18 of these books they found 261 pictures of males, but only 23 pictures of females. In close to one-third of these books women were not mentioned at all and those who were mentioned in the remaining two-thirds had no jobs or professions. In leadership roles, women were fairies or other mythical characters. A similar study examining the content of Swedish children's books showed boys in situations of knowledge, action, and intrigue; but girls were portrayed as being devoted to clothes and personal appearance.

An analysis of songs researched the content of six music texts used in schools in the Portland, Oregon, area (Gaspeed et al., 1973). These books contained a total of 773 songs, of which 16 per cent pertained to males and 6 per cent to females. Animals in male roles were described in 24 per cent of these songs, but in female roles only 6 per cent. The 773 songs mentioned a total of 30 male occupations, but only 7 female ones, the latter being cook, maid, mother, nurse, princess, queen, and witch.

It would seem relatively simple to remedy some of the above sex differences that exist in the schools. Reading texts and songbooks can be and are being written with a more equal proportion of male and female stories. Yet the question remains how much any educational policy should deviate from the social realities in which it functions. Would a credibility gap be set up if our grammar-school texts described the work of women dentists, women pilots, women truck drivers, and women fire fighters? Would it not be just as simple to actually train and employ women in these professions? Our schools are often blamed for not ameliorating social inadequacies that society at large is not willing to remedy. Integration in the United States would proceed much more smoothly if black and white adults were willing or able to move into each others' neighborhoods instead of trying to accomplish it by bussing their children. It is obvious that social change, be it integration or sex-role equalization, would best be accomplished if it took place inside as well as outside the school.

While the subject matter and the administration of grammar schools is heavily male oriented, the actual teaching is done predominantly by females. It has been postulated that some of the boys' learning difficulties are caused by a sex-role conflict, an expectancy to act masculine in a female dominated classroom. This hypothesis, however, has not been experimentally validated. The few experiments that have examined the relationship between sex of pupil and sex of teacher found no markable influences. Examining fifth grade students, Asher and Gottman (1974) report no significant effect of sex of teacher on female or male reading performance. Whether a class was taught by a male or female teacher, the girls had a superior reading performance. In the seventh and eighth grades, Good et al. (1973) found that the same sex differences existed in classes taught by females or males. The presence of a male teacher did not eliminate or reverse the sex differences found in a typical grammar-school class. Boys interacted more frequently with teachers of both sexes and received more positive and negative contacts from them. Good et al. believe that the teachers are primarily reactive to the differential behavior presented to them by boys and girls.

DISCUSSION

Small sex differences exist in specific intellectual functions. Females in general are slightly superior in verbal and memory tasks and there are indications that part of these skills may be inherited. Males in general perform better on spatial and arithmetical problems, especially after the age of puberty. Although these intellectual differences are small at the beginning, they become reinforced by the individuals themselves and by the cultural stereotypes leading males and females more and more into sex-specific educational and vocational directions.

To equalize intellectual differences, efforts should be made to occupy children of both sexes with both vocal and mechanical activities. On the grammar-school level, certain mental functions should be considered as part of the curriculum offering them in a compensatory way giving boys extra training in vocalization, detailed memory, and dexterity and giving girls extra practice in spatial orientation and arithmetical reasoning. This would require separate training sessions for boys and girls and it would further require that the training in these mental functions not be considered an elective. Such recommendations may appear undemocratic or unequal, but as has been pointed out, sex-roles tend to become more divergent if the choice is left to the boys and girls. One may wonder how a child, or an adult for that matter, can make an intelligent choice about a subject without some initial familiarity.

For some unknown reason, American schools require many more hours in English and social studies involving vocabulary and memory than in the sciences involving special orientation and arithmetic. Thus, there are more requirements in the female "superiority" areas than in the male areas of proficiency. This unequal requirement system "forces" the boys to take many hours of English, compensating them for their weaker intellectual areas, but the system does not "force" the girls to take science, which would compensate them in their weaker areas. Our educational ideas still have a classic flavor. One is considered educated if one knows literature and art whether or not one knows mathematics, physics, or chemistry. However, most of our high status professions require scientific knowledge, and it would seem logical to put equal emphasis on literature and science and require that both subjects are taken by both sexes.

Chapter 6

VOCATIONAL DIFFERENCES

Differences between the sexes are most obvious in the vocations. There are some areas of work that are predominantly carried out by women and others almost exclusively by men. There are also gross sex differences in hiring, classification, pay, and promotion procedures within and between various occupations, which in general discriminate against women. On examining the origin and the maintaining forces of these discriminations, two major questions arise. To which degree are the discriminations psychological and to which degree are they of an economic nature; and, secondly, whether they stem from the employee's or the employer's side. In this chapter we shall discuss some of the historical antecedents of the division of labor. We shall attempt to analyze the factors that motivate women to work and the vocational discriminations, they experience.

Origins of Sex-Specific Labor

Almost all anthropological accounts report a division of labor between men and women. In most cultures men did the hunting and fishing and women the gathering and the preparation of food. In agricultural societies the division of labor was less distinct with both females and males engaging at times in planting, gathering, and food preparation. Despite the sex-specific work there was a unity in the purpose of the work the individual family members performed, and much of this work was carried out in or near the home. This work pattern changed in the developed countries with the Industrial Revolution when families moved from the farms into the cities, where the place of work became separated from the home and only the man could leave the home since the woman was occupied with childbearing and child rearing. It has been estimated that women had an average of six children at that time; and before pasteurization, refrigeration, and adequate milk supplies for the cities almost all children had to be breast fed. Life expectancy was several decades shorter and childbearing and breast feeding filled the entire mature life span of many women, making work outside their home an impossibility (Judith Blake, 1974).

It is doubtful whether the biological factor of male strength played a role in sex discrimination in labor since the labor of weak children was sufficient to support the Industrial Revolution for a certain length of time. On the other hand, it is interesting to note that the muscle strength of women is 65 per cent that of men, and that women's earnings are also 65 per cent that of men. To accomplish a certain muscular work, two men are equivalent to three women, and in terms of pay two men receive as much as three women. There may have been some justification for this "economic" equation at a time when work was closely related to muscular strength. But there is no justification for a differential pay after the machines have taken over most of the hard labor and after muscular strength is no longer at a premium. Ironically, the low pay for women has spread into work areas that require speed and dexterity, capacities in which women seem to have a biological advantage. In such occupations as doing the laundry, food packing, knitting, and typing, women produce more than men, yet they receive only 70 per cent of the remuneration received by men working in these industries.

There are certain "protective enactment" laws that require special working conditions for women. They may have had a biological origin, although they differ from country to country. Some states of the United States prescribe that women lift no more than a specified amount (50 – 100 pounds) and have certain rest periods. In other countries women are prohibited from working in mines. Sweden repealed a law prohibiting women from working in mines and on night shifts and replaced it with strict regulations on these two types of work for both female and male workers (Gubbels, 1970). In Germany a woman cannot be discharged from any employment during pregnancy and for eight weeks thereafter. Employer and national health insurance share the cost of the continued salary for all absences during this period. While some women consider these "protective" measures as discriminatory, others believe that they are biologically and socially justified and can accept their benefits without feeling discriminated against.

It is difficult to know where biological origins end and psychological ones begin and to what degree technical events have influenced our thoughts and mores. A century or two ago there was no alternative but to believe that it is desirable for a woman to stay at home, bear children, and nurse them. As Judith Blake (1974) says, "we capitalize into a virtue what appeared to be a necessity." Once these virtues become established they are taught to the children who accept them as "natural" or "god given" and in turn teach them to their children. Beliefs are maintained even though the events for which they once served as rationalizations may no longer exist. In the 1970s women in the United States have only an average of two children, and 12 million (one-third of the women work force) work while they have preschool children. However, the necessity for women to work (if it is one) has not yet been capitalized into a virtue; the traditional views relating to women and home are still much in existence.

Female Work Motivation

Presumably the motives why single women work do not differ from those of single men, since three-fourths of both groups are employed. However, the work motivation for married women is more conflictual. We shall examine it in more detail, since the increase in the women's labor force has largely been an increase of women who are married. In the 1950s there were about 20 million women in the U.S. labor force and only 16 per cent of them were married. In the 1970s about 37 million women work in the United States and 41 per cent of them are married (*U.S. News & World Report*, 1975).

Several surveys taken in the early 1970s (National Fertility Study, 1970; Harris poll, 1972) found that the majority of single, married, and once-married women believed that it is better if the man provides and the woman cares for the home and family and said that they would like to have a "loving husband who would take care of them." Loving husbands and marriage, however, do not seem to keep married women from working and the attitudes do not seem to support the statistics. In the last two decades more women (17 million) than men (12 million) have joined the U.S. labor force and, as pointed out above, nearly half of these 17 million women are married.

There are also some conflictual data among the sexes themselves when they are asked the question why women work. In a study conducted in West Germany 85 per cent of the husbands stated that their wives worked in order to be able to contribute to building up the household, while only about 65 per cent of the wives held this same belief. A much larger percentage of the wives mentioned that they worked for psychological reasons (Simitis & Zenz, 1975). Reports from the Soviet Union also indicate some disharmony about the motives of female work. A survey taken in Leningrad showed that 75 per cent of the men consider their wives' work a "necessary evil" and the same survey found that only about 50 per cent of the families needed a second income (Butenschön, 1975).

Economists have also been concerned about the married woman's motivation to work. Janice Madden (1973) reports certain statistical "contradictions" with regard to work and the marital status of women. As income rises married women work more, but single women and men work less. It is also reported that at any given time a lower percentage of women work whose husbands have high earnings as compared to the percentage of women whose husbands earn less. This observation seems to contradict the trend that the income of husbands and the number of wives in the work force are both increasing.

In order to gain insight into the motives females have towards work, psychologists have examined a variety of demographic and attitudional data. Roxann Van Dusen and Eleanor Sheldon (1976) list some of the changes that have occurred in the life cycle of U.S. women and relate them to the increasing employment of women as follows: In the 1970s most working women are married; over two-thirds of them have child-rearing responsibilities in addition to their jobs; and more than half of them are over 40; they expect and have fewer children; they enter the family phase later, and they have become more often head of households through divorce, separation, nonmarriage, and through the general notion that marriage is not eternal, if at all necessary. Married women enter the labor force more often because they have more adequate schooling. They tend to postpone marriage and childbearing after marriage and find it more difficult to give up their economic independence after marriage. What has been termed the "life cycle squeeze" describes that most married women work early in their marriage when expenses are high and again late in their marriage when providing for growing children become necessary.

On the psychological side it has been postulated that married women work because they find it challenging and derive satisfaction from their jobs. Douglas Hall and Francine Gordon (1973) have studied the career choices of married women, their conflicts, their conformity, and their satisfactions. They gave questionnaires to 370 women asking them about their general happiness and satisfaction. They asked full-time housewives, part-time volunteer workers, as well as full-time and part-time employees. In each group there were women who did what they preferred to do and those who would rather do something else if given a chance.

It was found that full-time housewives who had indicated on the questionnaire that they preferred to do what they did scored high on a general satisfaction test; those who preferred to do something else scored low. One would expect such a positive correlation between a preferred activity and general satisfaction, but this correlation was not found for women working full time or part time. Women who worked and who had indicated on their questionnaire that they preferred it made the same average satisfaction score as those who had indicated that they did not prefer to work.

The above data indicate that a housewife's attitude about her housework is related to her general satisfaction, but that a working woman's attitude about her work has no such effect. Hall and Gordon suggest that it is easier to satisfy the choices of home-oriented women than the choices of work-oriented women. They point out that society gives stronger and less conflicting support to those women who want to be housewives than to those who want to work. The social forces that have motivated women to move from the homes into the offices have not supplied the accompanying satisfaction. There is dissatisfaction among those who want to get out of the home but are still in it, and there is dubious satisfaction for those who have got out of the home and have joined the work force. Lower pay, traditional attitudes, and additional housekeeping work offset much of the satisfaction gained by employment.

Adverse working conditions alone may not account for being dissatisfied with a job. In England, for instance, female physicians give up their practice after an average of seven years in favor of marriage or family. These professional women competed successfully with men for many years and one could assume that they would be wise to men and medicine and that neither financial needs nor unwanted pregnancies pushed them into marriage or family life. Since they have acted against sex-role stereotypy for most of their lives, it is difficult to know whether they finally yield to the cultural pressures or whether family life or the prospect of it may have a motivating power of its own as fulfilling as a professional career.

Educated women have been studied more than any other group. Eli Ginsberg (1966) reports on the life styles of over 300 graduates with professional careers. Many of those women expressed much satisfaction with their careers and experienced little or no conflict with regard to family and child rearing. Some of their responses were as follows: "I feel I must work to express myself regardless of my children's needs;" "I would work whether I was paid or not;" "I never dread the coming of a working day;" "I enjoy work and would be miserable sitting at home;" and "My children benefit from my absence and I am better tempered when I am home." Satisfaction in both the personal and the career areas was expressed by 72 per cent. It should be noted that the women questioned by Ginzburg belonged to a highly select group working in research or university settings with flexible work schedules and whose finances allowed for adequate child care. Their statements should be taken as ideal, picturing that which could happen if females had well-paid and interesting jobs, flexible schedules, and the availability of child-care facilities.

In general females are consistently less satisfied with work and retirement than are males, but Smith et al. (1969) found that gender is not the crucial factor. If groups of men are compared with groups of women who have similar jobs, equal pay, and promotional opportunities, then their satisfaction rating as measured by the "Job Description Index" will also be more similar.

Half the women employed full time do not want to be employed full time. Many of them desire part-time employment and about one-fourth of all women who do work are part-time workers. It seems logical that a part-time job would be a compromise between staying at home and working full time, although it apparently creates more conflicts than it solves. Part-time employees in Hall and Gordon's study reported lower satisfaction than those who preferred housework, volunteer work, or full-time employment, yet the majority of women prefer part-time work to any other activity. Of those actually working part time only 19 per cent said that they would prefer a change, while 51 per cent of the housewives and 45 per cent of those with full-time employment indicated a desire to change.

Hall and Gordon try to explain this conflict between being "dissatisfied" with part-time work and yet "preferring" it by speculating that part-time work is often not challenging and yet appealing because it solves nonworking. They also suggest that part-time work may not solve internal conflicts as it was observed that many part-time workers were also involved in full-time housework and in additional volunteer work. The satisfaction reported by the female part-time worker is also related to her educational level. Spreitzer et al. (1975) found that a high degree of happiness was reported by only 27 per cent of the group with 12 or fewer years of schooling but by 49 per cent of those with 13 or more years schooling. They also found that among the more educated part-time workers there were twice as many (72 per cent) who perceived their life as more exciting.

The motivation for women to work cannot be fully assessed without considering the discrimination they experience at work, yet it is impossible to pinpoint the conditions responsible for unequal employment practices. Discriminations occur on the supply as well as on the demand side of the female labor market. Employers exclude women from certain jobs, pay them less, and promote them less frequently. They do not consider these inequities as discriminatory since they frequently counter that female employees are inadequately prepared, work less regularly, and avoid certain jobs. There is also discrimination on the public's and the trade unions' part preferring certain male products and services.

Supply Discrimination

It has been pointed out in a previous chapter that females are channeled and allowed to drift away from the technical and scientific fields toward the clerical and humanitarian services. This development begins preschool and continues throughout the entire educational process. At the end of an educational phase, whether high school or college, there are fewer women than men with technical skills and interests, a factor that limits the choices of the female employee as well as those of the prospective employer. The obvious answer to this limitation—advocated by Betty Friedan and many others—is an equal education, which will prepare females for the same range of occupations as it prepares males.

However, equal education does not seem to be the sole answer to pay equality. There seems to be an educational "paradox" with respect to female employees. In analysing women's pay, Fuchs (1971) has shown that women in the food canning and similar industries earn 69 per cent of the wages men earn; but in accounting and bookkeeping, which require more schooling, they earn only 44 per cent of the salary men earn. Swiss census figures of 1972 show also that women who perform skilled labor get 65 per cent of the wages of their male counterparts, while women who perform unskilled work receive 70 per cent of the male wage. Thus the amount of training a job requires seems to widen, rather than close, the pay gap between the male-female differential.

Viewed over a period of time, there is also a contradiction with respect to education and pay. Women have increased their educational standards. The percentage of female high school graduates with some college has risen from 24 per cent in 1940 to 46 per cent in 1974, and in 1971 women earned 42 per cent of all bachelor of arts degrees awarded and 40 per cent of all master of arts. In spite of these educational advances, the earnings gap between men and women has been widening instead of closing. Women holding full-time jobs in 1974 averaged $6,800 per year, 43 per cent less than the $11,800 per year earned by men. Twenty years prior this differential was smaller: 36 per cent (*U.S. News and World Report*, 1975).

Aside from an imbalance in education, the "fear of success" has often been thought to hinder a woman's chance for equal employment. Eleanor MacDonald, director of a London employment agency, advertised for a woman to fill a post for a salary of $8,400 per year but received no bids. When she readvertised the job with a salary of $3,360, she received many calls (*Time* magazine, 1974). Incidents like this may have led psychologists to hypothesize that women have a tendency to avoid success and are negatively motivated toward status jobs because they may experience a conflict between career and home life.

In 1968 Matina Horner postulated that women view femininity and achievement as two desirable but opposing motives. In order to measure how much women tend to avoid success in intellectual leadership and competence Horner designed a test that presented the following written leads to a story her subjects had to complete: "After first term finals *Anne* finds herself at the top of her medical school class." and "After first term finals *John* finds himself at the top of his medical school class." In Horner's experiments, and in a number of subsequent ones based on her method, it was found that a large majority of women predicted a dim future for Anne but not for John. In an experiment comparing Australian and U.S. college students Feather and Raphelson (1974) found that both Australian and U.S. males wrote a greater proportion of fear-of-success stories to the Anne than to the John lead. So did the females in the Australian sample, but the U.S. females wrote about an equal amount of fear-of-success stories to the two leads. The authors suggest the possible influence of the women's liberation movement on the U.S. females.

A large number of fear-of-success experiments were conducted, but their results became more and more equivocal. Tresemer (1974) reviewed the subject in an article entitled "Fear of success: popular but unproven." Examining 61 studies, he found that the proportion of women writing fear-of-success stories varied from 11 per cent to 88 per cent, and that the proportions of males writing fear of success stories was similar, ranging from 14 per cent to 86 per cent. Lois Hoffman (1974) reports that the percentage of females writing fear-of-success stories remained constant between 1965 and 1971, while the fear-of-success responses of the males rose from 8 per cent in 1965 to 77 per cent in 1971. The common theme for females in 1971 was an "affiliative loss" because of success, while males questioned the value of achievement. The Australian comparison suggested that U.S. women, but not the U.S. males, have been positively influenced by the liberation movement, while Hoffman's data indicate that the women have not changed, but that the fear-of-success responses of the men have greatly increased. The results of experiments involving imagination and the prediction of the future are in general not very reliable, and the fear-of-success experiments seem to be greatly influenced by rather temporary political and socioeconomic changes.

A more concrete approach to the fear-of-success problem is presented by Richard Sorrentino and Judith-Ann Short (1974). They compared the fear-of-success scores of their subjects with the success on an actual performance task. They found that women with a high fear of success performed better on a task when it had a masculine label, such as "Tracing Architectual Forms" than when it was femininely labeled "Pattern and Design Tracing." These data show that the very fear of success can be of benefit in the actual performance of certain tasks and that the experience of this fear (if it exists) should in no way preclude the actual success in training for a career or in the career itself.

Demand Discrimination

The variables on the female employee's side can only be partially responsible for the employment inequality. On the employer's side women are often considered as the "cake winner" and believed to have high turnover and sickleave rates. However, a number of U.S. and British reports indicate that turnover and sickleave percentages are almost equal if we compare men and women in equal job categories, for example, female cannery workers with male cannery workers, female teachers with male teachers, etc. (U.S. Civil Service Commission, 1972; British Department of Employment, 1975). Lyle and Ross (1973) point out that few companies have sex-specific records on absenteeism and that the management complains just as often of losing "bright, young" men to competitors as they complain of females leaving employment.

Employers have often stereotyped ideas of female and male character traits and discriminate accordingly to match job specifications. Rosen and Jerdee (1974 a) examined the effects of an applicant's sex and the hiring for managerial position in the clothing business. In a simulated situation they had 235 business majors judge male and female applications for executive positions. The job demands for some of the positions required "aggressive interpersonal behavior and decisive managerial action" and for others "routine clerical accuracy and dependable performance." Only 46 per cent of the female applicants were accepted for the aggressive and decisive position, but 72 per cent for the routine and dependable one. The corresponding acceptance figures for males were 65 per cent and 76 per cent. It should be noted that the discrimination for the "aggressive" position was not 100 per cent. Almost half the women were accepted for the aggressive and decisive position as compared to two-thirds of the men. This shows that women should not be discouraged by higher rejection rates, but should counteract them by implementing more frequent job applications. Such strategy may be necessary until the employment opportunities are equal for both sexes.

Discrimination is often quite specific to the branch of business, to positions, and to tasks. Hamner et al. (1974) investigated the sex variable in the performance of store clerks. They showed film strips to potential grocery store managers in which male and female employees stacked "number 10" cans onto shelves. The employees wore the same clothing and had training in stacking cans. Various three-minute film strips showed a high performance group stacking 48 cans, an average performance group stacking 36 cans, and a low performance group stacking 24 cans. In all three performance groups female stackers were rated higher than male stackers by both female and male raters, although in actuality males and females stacked the same number of cans in each performance group. The females in the highest performance group, those stacking 48 cans per three minutes, received the highest ratings. The authors believe that females are rated higher when they perform a "male" task.

The vast majority of women, however, work in "feminine" jobs where there is frequent discrimination in evaluation and promotion procedures as shown, for example, in a study by Rosen and Jerdee (1974 b). In this study 95 male bank supervisors were asked to decide on the promotion of bank employees. They were given identical service and job descriptions for both sexes, differing only in the male or female name. Under these "equal" conditions the supervisors promoted 19 out of 49 women, but 32 out of 44 men. In the same study the supervisors approved "leave of absence" more frequently for women than for male employees, indicating again the stereotype that men should be more dedicated to their jobs than women. The discrimination ratio, promoting about half the women and about three quarters of the male applicants, is similar to the percentages of discrimination reported by Rosen and Jerdee for the hiring of managerial personnel for the clothing industry.

Cumulative Discrimination

Economists have difficulties ascribing all the discrimination to supply and demand factors. They define as "cumulative" those discriminations based on general, cultural customs and on the specific attitudes of the consumer. In their business relations men seem to like men better than women, but women do not seem to reciprocate their dislike—they also prefer men to women. In a survey in Switzerland 50 per cent of the female employees indicated they preferred male supervisors, 20 per cent preferred females, and 30 per cent reported no preference (Held & Levy, 1974). In a U.S. study the attitudes of males and females toward a high prestige job (civil engineer) and a low prestige job (custodian) were examined by Suchner and More (1975). Both jobs were described once as being executed by a "Mr." so-and-so and once by a "Mrs." so-and-so. They were to be rated on an activity, friendliness, intelligence, etc. scale. Both males and females rated the civil engineers (Mr. and Mrs. versions) as more brainy, and the custodian (Mr. and Mrs.) as more likable. Males did not differentiate their ratings of people by sex, but female raters found the males more likable than the females in the high-prestige as well as in the low-prestige occupations. As in the Swiss survey, the females acknowledged the competence of female executives by giving them high intelligence ratings but indicated by their low "likable" ratings that they would rather not work under them.

Fuchs (1971) has analyzed the pay differential of males and females and finds that discrimination cannot be ascribed to any specific group of employers. He presents U.S. data from the early 1960s in which 46 industries were surveyed with respect to the different wages and salaries they paid their female and male employees. These data show that women as compared to men earned the least (only 28 per cent of that what men earned) in certain health-care jobs in nursing and convalescent homes and proportionally the most (88 per cent of the men's salary) working in barber and beauty shops.

Looking at the salary in absolute terms, women as well as men get the lowest salary in those industries where there are predominantly women and the highest salary where there are predominantly men. Of the 46 industries and businesses listed by Fuchs, the hourly wages were highest in the legal services, advertising, newspaper publishing, aircraft and parts, motor vehicles and equipment—in occupations with relatively few women. The hourly wages were the lowest in occupations with the largest proportions of women workers: variety stores, laundry and cleaning, eating and drinking, knitting mills, and canning and preserving. In 1973 the gross hourly income for U.S. textile workers with a high percentage of women was $2.94 and that for the building trade with relatively few women was $5.40.

Similar trends occur in other countries. In Switzerland the average monthly wage in the textile and clock industries where women are in the majority is 1,400 Swiss francs, but in the building industry with few women the average monthly salary is 1,800 Swiss francs. In West Germany these differences are less pronounced although they are in the same direction. Women in the food industry, where they outnumber men three to one, earn about 1,000 Deutsche Mark per month. In the textile industry, in which they represent about half of the workers, they earn 1,100 Deutsche Mark per month, and in the building industry, in which there are only 4 per cent women, they earn 1250 Deutsche Mark (Statistisches Jahrbuch, 1975).

Fuchs does not consider discrimination by employers and supervisors as major factors. If it was, he reasons, the differences among government employees ought to be the largest, because there are many bosses and supervisors. The differences among the self-employed ought to be the smallest, because there are no employers and supervisors. But the data show clearly that the male-female differential is the largest for the self-employed and the smallest for government employees. Fuchs suspects that the great difference between the self-employed males and females is due to customer discrimination. For example, most males and females would prefer a male rather than a female mechanic to work on their car regardless of the female mechanic's training or experience. Fuchs finds equally large male-female differentials in union and nonunion industries as well as in small and large businesses and industries. He therefore concludes that no single group is responsible for this differential and that it is the customer or the society as a whole causing the male-female pay inadequacies. He believes equalization will require the combined efforts of men and women at home and in school as well as in business and industry.

Another factor frequently thought to be responsible for the lower pay of females is the "crowding hypothesis." It consists of hiring women (also minorities) for only a limited number of occupations to create competition, oversupply, and an acceptance of lower wages. Crowding is a fact. Two thirds of all employed women work in only seven occupations: secretarial, retail sales, households, teaching, bookkeeping, waitress, and nursing. Of all the female professionals, over 50 per cent crowd into just two professions —elementary teaching and registered nursing (Fuchs, 1975). Lower pay for the female occupations is also a fact as Fuchs's analysis has shown.

Although there is a correlation, crowding and lower pay are not necessarily causally related. Crowding can also be observed in socialist countries where female and male workers receive equal pay. In the Soviet Union 96 per cent of the textile workers, 85 per cent of the health-service personnel, and 76 per cent of the food handlers are women (Butenschön, 1975). Since we cannot infer any ulterior motives of lower pay on the employer's part, we should therefore consider such psychological factors as modeling or "herding" as a possible explanation. This simply means that women may want to work where other women work independent of financial considerations.

It has also been pointed out by Lyle and Ross (1973) that the industries with a large proportion of women—textiles, social services, and food handling—were the ones that expanded most rapidly in the last decades while there was a larger pool of unemployed females than males available.

Because women's specialties are associated with low pay in our society, we are reluctant to accept the hypothesis that women perform better and feel more comfortable at tasks involving certain types of manual dexterity. It would be interesting to know if Soviet textile workers feel discriminated against because their industry is almost exclusively feminine. If crowding is not related to pay, but merely to production goals, then women's specialties could be experienced as an advantage rather than a disadvantage.

Equalization Efforts

As discussed in Chapter 1, different women's liberation groups advocate different approaches to reach equalization. The suggestion of masculinization for women and feminization for men would eventually accomplish an equal sex distribution within the vocations, while the aims of the womanhood movement would bring about more crowding. Socialists and Marxists, on the other hand, are primarily concerned about equal pay and not necessarily about an equal distribution of the sexes within the vocations. The success of these various approaches cannot be evaluated because their methods are relatively new and occur in an economic system undergoing changes within itself.

The most consistent equalization efforts in the United States came in the form of governmental legislation. From 1962 when President John F. Kennedy ordered an end to sex bias in hiring and promoting federal employees, there has been continued legislation towards vocational equality with respect to pay, job classification, the granting of credits, and jury duty and pregnancy pay. Despite these regulations the male-female pay differential has increased in the last two decades. In 1956 women earned 63 per cent of the men's pay; in 1964 59 per cent and in 1974 only 57 per cent (*U.S. News and World Report,* 1975).

Robert Moran (1970) describes certain variables and discriminatory practices that have hindered pay equality. He points out that the Equal Pay Act of 1963 was passed by Congress because it was incorporated into the Fair Labor Standards Act, thereby covering only about half the jobs in the United States, excluding state and local government jobs, domestic employment, outside salespersons, and all higher paying jobs not subject to the wage and hour law. Another difficulty in administering the act is the word "equal," which was defined as not necessarily meaning "identical." Does this mean that a woman who packs headache pills must get the same wages than a man who inspects them at the end of the line, or vice versa; and how about the male and female chemists who work on the composition of these pills. The courts have difficulties defining steps as equal or unequal if they pertain to the production of a single product.

Moran cites other discriminatory loopholes such as the "heavy lifting" claim, which has been used to avoid equal pay. Male jobs are occasionally specified to require heavy lifting, something that makes them unequal, although in actuality there is no heavy lifting required. Another way out is the alleged management training program where a man doing a bank teller's job, for instance, is classified as a management trainee. The woman doing the same job is simply classified as a bank teller employee. From 1963 to 1970 the courts handled 50,000 cases involving underpayment of women with claims totaling 17 million dollars. Moran states that in spite of the courts' efforts and many voluntary adjustments by employers and unions, women continue to be underemployed in a variety of establishments.

In 1972 the U.S. Equal Employment Opportunity Commission was empowered to pursue court action in discrimination cases where voluntary efforts were unsuccessful. But Virginia Pendergrass et al. (1976) point out that the litigation process is often a lonely, expensive, and emotionally trying experience for the woman and they offer technical advice and suggest sex-discrimination counseling during this period. They advise that institutional grievance committees and local and state offices should first be consulted before complaints are filed with federal agencies. They also describe the personal dynamics involved in discrimination, how to recognize them, and how and where to get personal counseling during discrimination actions.

More long-term equalization efforts are described by Oonagh Hartnett (1975) pointing to the responsibilities of occupational psychologists to disseminate the results of studies which show that women are dependable and suitable for leadership jobs and that their turnover rate when treated equally is no higher than the rate for males. Similar to the compensatory education programs in the United States, Hartnett suggests special curricula devised for boys and girls who have not been exposed to basic physics. Such programs may put girls on an equal footing with boys in the more technical areas, such as appliance repair and motor mechanics.

DISCUSSION

An attempt has been made to look historically at some of the biological antecedents that may have caused the division of labor between men and women. Whether these factors were a matter of physical strength or of childbearing they have lost much of their functional survival value, and yet society has not fully accepted the idea that women—and especially married women—should work outside the home. This puts many women in a conflict situation which is compounded by the fact that women earn about 40 per cent less than men.

The discrimination women experience in low pay, lower job classifications, and in fewer promotions seem to stem from several causes—from inadequate education, from possible crowding into female professions, and from prejudice with regard to leadership abilities, dependability, and absenteeism.

A better and more advanced education does not guarantee higher pay for women. It may widen the gap through crowding and competition if the education is obtained in predominantly female areas such as teaching and nursing.

On the positive side it should be noted that discrimination is not an all-or-none phenomenon but rather a matter of degree, and some additional efforts on the woman's part (not justified, but practical) may give her equal employment chances. There are also some employment situations where the discrimination is against men in favor of women. Women in almost all levels of employment will earn the most if they avoid the traditional female areas and enter the male ones—if, for example, they sell automobile parts rather than ladies' apparel.

Possibilities for equalization through legal channels have also been discussed as well as the tasks of the educator and vocational psychologist to increase the females' scientific and technical knowledge and to dispel prejudices related to employment.

Chapter 7

SEXUAL ACTIVITIES

Sex is perhaps the one area in which there is a definite natural difference between men and women. Differences in physiology account for differences in behaviors and feelings during intercourse. Yet, there are a variety of behaviors caused by the rules of dating and by the aesthetics involved in partner selection for which our culture gives us more-or-less specific models. In this chapter we shall attempt to discuss various theories and observational data that describe the development of the sexual urge giving special emphasis to Freud's theory on female sexuality and to criticisms of it derived from empirical studies. Several surveys about the sexual activities of adolescents and adults will be reviewed in order to assess the feelings, desires, and habits of males and females during their sexual activities.

It is still a big question whether any individual can have sexual feelings before the onset of puberty or before menstruation or ejaculation can occur. Even experienced adults have difficulty communicating the quality of their sexual feelings, and it is difficult to know what a child or a preadolescent experiences when performing or imitating a sexual act. In spite of this difficulty, theories that ascribe to young children all sorts of sexual experiences flourish, most notably Freud's theory, which assumes that infantile "sexual" experiences differ for boys and girls influencing their personalities and behaviors for a lifetime.

Freudian Sex

Sigmund Freud (1856–1939) was one of the first who wrote about sexual urges and feelings, considering them natural aspects of life. Over a period of 40 years he wrote about 350 books, articles, and monographs totaling more than 8,000 pages. He wrote in an abstract and involved manner, in perhaps the only way acceptable to the Victorian mores of his time. His teachings about sex and psychic events have been widely accepted in Western countries because he was the first to write about sexual desires prolifically and with great literary skill. His doctrines seem to have filled an intellectual gap created by the outgoing religious beliefs and the not-yet-accepted science at the turn of the century. Because Freud wrote much in metaphors and because of his reliance on the "unconscious," research psychologists have had difficulties disproving many of his assumptions. The most urgent rejection of his ideas on the sexual development and the sexual status of females has come from women's liberation groups, including a number of female psychoanalysts. Following is a brief review of Freud's main assumption with respect to the sexual development of females and males.

Freud thought that the driving force or the energy of life, the "libido," is of a sexual nature and manifests itself through the various "psychosexual" stages. He named the first of these stages, which he thought lasted from birth to about two years, the "oral" stage. During that stage an infant satisfies desires by stimulating the mouth through sucking and eating nutritional as well as nonnutritional objects. In the second stage, the "anal" stage, believed to last from age two to four, desires and urges are supposedly satisfied through urination and defecation. During the third stage, the "phallic" stage, assumed to last from the fourth to the seventh year, desires are satisfied through manipulation of the genital areas.

Freud went on to postulate that all oral, anal, and phallic urges must be satisfied during their respective periods, so that a normal personality and a normal adult sex life can develop. He assumed, for instance, that there is an innate sucking urge that must be satisfied, or "come out," during the oral period. Should this urge not be satisfied during this period it will increase and will manifest itself in later life through excessive eating, drinking, smoking, talking—through any activity involving the mouth—something Freud related to "oral personality." One may wonder what is sexual about eating and why Freud considered eating as something "psychosexual." In Freud's system, however, sex is very broadly defined, meaning something like life-energy, propagation, or the survival of the species. Sex in his system could mean anything necessary to maintain life.

Freud considered human sexuality as "bi-phasic." Sexuality appears first in the psychosexual stages from 0 to 7 years and a second time in the genital period that begins at puberty. He called this interim period from 7 years to puberty the "latency" period, and he believed that sexual urges were dormant during these years. Freud's "genital" period starts at puberty and was subdivided into stages of narcissism, homosexuality, and heterosexuality. In other words, it is considered normal for an adolescent to go successively through the stages of self-love, homosexuality, and heterosexual love. Repressions of an unconscious nature can occur at any time during the genital period similar to those described in the discussion of the oral and anal stages. A homosexual, for instance, who has never had heterosexual relations is termed a "fixated" homosexual, while one who did engage in heterosexual activities is considered a "regressed" homosexual, implying that the homosexual phase was not satisfied and hence the desires to return to it increased. The essential dynamic relationship between the suppression of urges and the resulting maladjustments are considered equal for both sexes. Females as well as males are said to go through oral, anal, and phallic stages, through the latency period, and through the genital periods of narcissism, homosexuality, and heterosexuality.

Other Freudian postulations about the dynamics of sex contain distinct sex differences. In early childhood, for instance, a boy is said to fall in love with his mother and considers his father as a rival and therefore hates him (the Oedipus complex). As he hates his father he becomes afraid of possible reprisals, fearing in particular that his father will cut off his penis. To forestall this action and to counteract his fears, the boy turns about and loves his father (the Castration complex). Thus, in Freud's system, love and hate become interdependent: the more the boy hates his father, the more he fears the father's reprisal and the more he will love him.

Freud imagined that the girl's route to her sexual development is much more difficult and he suggested involved hypotheses to "explain" this development. Like a boy, a girl initially loves her mother (Oedipus or pre-Oedipus), but discovers soon that her brother or her father has a penis and she blames her mother for having produced her with imperfect body parts. Moreover, the girl fantasizes that she had a penis but lost it through castration—a fantasy that creates feelings of bodily inferiority in her (the Castration complex). Out of this dislike for the mother the girl turns to the father as the love object. She also begins to identify with the mother as a competitor. To overcome her inferiority resulting from the lack of a penis, the girl wishes to be impregnated and to have a baby. Her changing of love objects from mother to father and her wish for impregnation require her to transfer the focal point of her pleasure away from the phallic zone, the clitoris, toward the receptive organ, the vagina. This in turn requires an accompanying change in personality away from the active, masculine, and aggressive clitoral stimulation toward the passive, subordinate, masochistic—toward receiving vaginal stimulation. The change of the female's love object from the mother to the father brings with it a love-hate relationship similar to that of the male. However, the reasons for this relationship are assumed to be different. The female is in love with the father for the above stated reasons (the Electra complex), and the more she loves him the more she wants to be like him and the more she hates him, because she cannot be like him since he has a penis and she has not (the Penis Envy complex).

Freud considered the clitoral-vaginal shift as a necessary condition for normal, female sexuality. He states that a girl, unlike a boy, should not manually stimulate her genitals too often during her phallic period (4–7 years) because she should not accustom herself to receiving pleasure from her "stunted" penis, her clitoris. If she does receive this "masculine" pleasure in her childhood it may lead to homosexuality, inferiority, or to frigidity because her clitoris may refuse to give up its pleasure during puberty when the clitoral sensitivity is to be replaced in favor of vaginal sensitivity. Here Freud postulated the learning of a habit, not congruent with his general view that urges dissipate when they become satisfied.

In summary, the female as compared to the male has a number of disadvantages in the Freudian system: a psychic inferiority involving body parts, a faulty conscience (super-ego), a psychic love-hate ambivalence toward the opposite sex, and guilt feelings because she had to change her love from her mother to her father. All this, according to Freud, makes the female predisposed to envy, to an inadequate sense of justice, and to an incapability to substitute desirable actions for undesirable ones (sublimation). Freud believed that masculinity is basic for both sexes and that feminine sexuality is derived from masculine sexuality through complicated and hurdlesome routes (Freud: Collected Papers 1892–1939).

Critique on Freudianism

Freud's view on the secondary nature of female sexuality has been discredited by advanced biological knowledge and empirical studies. Mary Jane Sherfey (1966) points out that there is no scientific basis for Freud's "Eve-out-of-Adam" myth. She further states that embryos are morphologically females during the first weeks of fetal life. If the fetal gonads were removed before the fifth or sixth week all embryos would develop as females. Sherfey believes it would be more correct to say that the penis is an exaggerated clitoris, that the scrotum is derived from the labia minor, and that the original sex or gender is feminine. Modern embryology may call for an "Adam-out-of-Eve" concept. Other investigators (Money & Ehrhardt, 1972) state likewise that in the absence of fetal gonadal hormones the fetus always continues to differentiate the reproductive anatomy of the female. Testicular hormones are necessary for the development of the male reproductive system. If these hormones are present, the testes begin to develop during the seventh week; if they are not present the ovaries begin to develop a week later (Hutt, 1972).

Freud, who is generally hailed as a great theoretical innovator, may have merely reflected the cultural bias of his time when he theorized that the woman's sex and psyche are derived from man. He may have theorized that vaginal rather than clitoral stimulation was the normal and mature sex because he was a man and derived more pleasure from vaginal intercourse. He had no objective data on the clitoral-vaginal comparison, and, of course, no subjective experience. Data collected by Kinsey et al. (1953) show that only 18 out of 900 women were not responsive to clitoral stimulation. Those data are in opposition to Freud's assumptions. Kinsey et al. and Masters and Johnson (1966) suggest that all orgasms in women are directly or indirectly based on clitoral stimulation, while Fisher (1973) found that many of his subjects could report qualitative differences between the two modes of stimulation with 28 per cent reporting that clitoral stimulation is ecstatic and contributes more than vaginal stimulation. Only 6 per cent expressed a perference for vaginal stimulation. The remaining subjects expressed no preference including about 15 per cent who never achieved orgasm.

Although details are difficult to define in the Freudian system, certain general conclusions derived from his theory have been disproved by empirical studies. It has already been mentioned that Freud has been found wrong in assuming biological inferiority for females. There is also evidence against some of the psychological inferiority he ascribed to women. As pointed out previously, Nancy Bayley (1968) found females more resilient toward environmental influences and many other studies have reported greater adjustment difficulties for boys than for girls (Lynn, 1969; Hartley et al., 1962; Kohlberg, 1966). Some experimenters have found that boys have more anxiety about bodily damage and feel less secure than girls (Fisher, 1970). These results are contrary to the Freudian postulates regarding the woman's bodily inferiority. It is also known that stuttering, dyslexia (reading difficulty), hyperactivity, and bed-wetting occur about five times as often in boys as in girls. The Freudians assume that these difficulties are symptoms of underlying disturbances, but this is incongruent with their own theory that females have more disturbances and adjustment problems.

It is true, as many studies have shown, that women in North America and Western Europe have higher rates of certain mental illnesses than men. But Gove & Tudor (1973) who analyzed these studies found that it is primarily the married woman who has the higher incident rate. For the never-married, the divorced, and the widowed groups the majority of studies show a higher mental illness rate for men. With respect to mental illness, marriage seems to be more protective for males than for females. This is concurrent with the statistics that divorced men remarry more often than divorced women (he for the third, she for the second!). Another social factor that influences mental illness is employment. Leonore Radloff (1975) reports that unemployed married men are more depressed than unemployed married women. It has also been suggested that the higher rates of mental illness for females are propagated by male doctors who diagnose certain physical and social conditions as mental illness following the stereotypy of the weak, dependable, emotional, illogical, etc. woman. All these findings suggest that the higher rate of female mental illness is due to social factors and not as Freud believed to the female's sexual experiences during infancy.

Further evidence against the Freudian assumption comes from psychopathology. Freud believed that neuroses are due to unconscious childhood frustrations of a sexual nature, and he thought neurotic women to be sexually inhibited and less active. A number of experiments reviewed by Fisher (1973) suggest the opposite. There is evidence that normal sexual relationships are experienced by psychologically maladjusted women. Lea Schaefer (1964) found a full range of sexual responsiveness in the 30 neurotic women she examined. All women in her sample reported normal sex and orgasms. Schaefer believed that other investigators who were men obtained different results because their women patients were not as "open" during the interviews.

Freud did not consider experimental controls. He dealt mainly with neurotic women patients in a particular culture and inferred basic human mechanisms from what they told him occurred during their early childhood. There was no questioning of parents or relatives, nor were any records consulted to verify the patients' early experiences. In his entire lifetime Freud analyzed only one child, little Hans, and in this case Hans's father did much of the talking (Eysenck, 1968). Sigusch, who has reviewed 775 studies in his summary on the *Sexual Reaction of Women* (1971), states that psychoanalysts have no statistically significant data that can prove their arguments, not even enough data to warrant the formulation of hypotheses. Several female psychoanalysts, notably Therese Benedeck, Helene Deutsch, Karen Horney, Mary Jane Sherfey, and Clara Thompson (Fisher, 1973), disagree with Freud's idea that clitoral excitation must be given up in preference to vaginal for the obtainment of normal, sexual adulthood. Why these psychoanalysts reject Freud's clitoral-vaginal transfer theory, but accept many of his other assumptions that are just as speculative, is not clear.

The present account has dealt with the Freudian hypotheses concerning the development of female sex. Freud's postulations in other areas also lack experimental verification as, for instance, his concepts of the dynamics of the human mind (id, ego, super-ego, dreams, and symbolism), the various periods (psychosexual, latency, genital), as well as his ideas about the sexual development of males. The Oedipus-castration complexes are as undefinable for males as they are for females. Should a boy express hate towards his father, for instance, the analyst would invoke the Oedipus complex as an explanation. Should the boy express love toward his father, the Oedipus complex would also be considered as the cause, since the analyst would say that the boy was hiding his hate behind his love. In the Freudian system the man as well as the woman is doomed to a "dualistic catchall."

Behavioristic Views

There have been other hypotheses on infantile sex and love. The American behaviorist J.B. Watson (1917) thought that an infant can only experience three different types of emotions—love, rage, and fear—and that love, a precursor of sex, was elicited when an infant's erogenous zones were stroked or gently touched. As the child develops, voices and visual impressions become associated with the original stroking and the love-sex experiences turn into highly complex social behavior. Harlow (1959), experimenting with monkeys, has shown that infant monkeys need contact with either a natural mother or an artificial one that is warm and soft. Harlow's work has partially supported Watson's skin stroking hypothesis and many therapists believe maladjusted children and adults did not receive enough "contact love" in their early childhood. Therapeutic fads speak of positive "strokes" and encounter groups engage in the touching of hands and other parts of the body to make up for the emotion supposedly not received during or since childhood.

It is doubtful whether the need for "contact love" can be generalized to all infants and especially to all adults. Experimentation about contact love in humans has been limited. Those experiments carried out indicate that not all humans may require it. H.R. Schaffer and Peggy Emerson (1964) studied 37 infants very intensively, the care and treatment they received from their mothers as well as their mothers' personalities and social setting. They found that 19 infants, the "cuddlers," enjoyed being held, cuddled, or stroked; that nine others, the "noncuddlers," reacted against it; and that another nine could take it or leave it. These differences were observed from birth and it was found that neither the mother's personality nor the sex of the infant determined whether the infant was a cuddler or a noncuddler. Data like these, which suggest innate differences, have not found much acceptance in our "mother-blaming" society (Nash, 1970). The noncuddlers seem to depend more on eye contact, and it is quite possible that there are innate differences between tactile and visual stimulation preferences and that it would be better for some infants if they received a minimal amount of bodily contact.

Kinsey et al. (1953) distinguished between a physiological and a psychological orgasm and report that male children can have erections, body tenseness, increased breathing, and a sudden quiescence—reactions that resemble adult orgasm in all respects except in the actual ejaculation which does not occur. In preadolescence, between the ages of eight and fourteen, Kinsey et al. report an increase in sexual play among boys. This would contradict the Freudian "latency" period, in which sexual play is said to be dormant. It may have appeared as a period of inactivity to Freud because by the age of eight children may have learned to hide their sex play from parents and psychoanalysts successfully!

Kinsey et al. obtained their data on preadolescent sex from the memory of adults and also from adults who were sexually involved with children. Although erotic feelings and emotions were reported, it is not clear how much of this "psychological" orgasm was retrospectively inferred. Kinsey and his co-workers suggest that both physiological and psychological sex are diffuse during preadolescence and that children of that age are arousable by a wide variety of physical and mental conditions that become more narrow during adolescence and postadolescence, when more specific acts and conditions of arousal are required.

Compared to Freud's postulates, the behavioristic hypotheses are much simpler and can at times be experimentally tested. However, feelings and emotions are difficult to define and to assess, particularly if they pertain to children. Thus little is known of how children actually feel during those manifestations that psychologists call infantile love, sex, and orgasm. Experimentally, childhood love is a virgin field—as perhaps it should be!

Adolescence

During adolescence, sex-specific physiological changes become "superimposed" on already existing sex-role stereotypy. These physiological changes can be thought of creating sexual urges whose mode of satisfaction will depend a great deal on cultural modeling and environmental circumstances. Thus adolescence is a period in which physiology interacts with culture in crystallizing sex differences.

The first extensive and objective survey on adolescent sex was conducted by Michael Schofield as reported in his book *The Sexual Behavior of Young People* (1965). It is based on interviews of almost 2,000 English youths of all socioeconomic classes and presents many interesting data on the differences and similarities of the sexual practices of adolescents between the ages 15 and 19.

Somewhat contrary to expectations, it was found that most adolescents do not engage in intercourse and that only 20 per cent of the boys and 12 per cent of the girls practiced it. This incongruency in percentage was due to the fact that adolescent girls experienced sex more often with different partners than did adolescent boys. Two-thirds of the girls had their first intercourse with partners older than they, including one third who were introduced to sex by male adults. But only 2 per cent of the boys were introduced to sex by female adults, and, as Schofield states, "the proselytising older woman in search of virgin boys is either a myth, or very unsuccessful." Little is known about the effect of the age of the first sex partner. One can assume that the initial intercourse experience has a strong effect on future sexual desires and habits.

When asked for the motive of their first intercourse most boys indicated a "sexual desire," while the girls' predominant response was "being in love." Only half the girls who permitted having their genitals stimulated reciprocated in touching the boy's penis. The girls were, however, less passive when it came to the frequency of intercourse. Once the girls did have intercourse they had it again sooner and twice as often, 40 times per year, as compared to the boys who practiced it 20 times per year.

A decade later Schlaegel et al. (1975) studied sexual attitudes and practices of youths between 11 and 16 years old in northern West Germany. They found that certain behaviors such as kissing, dating, and having a friend were practiced almost equally often by males and females. Intercourse was experienced twice as often by 16-year-old girls (40 per cent) as by 16-year-old boys (22 per cent). In comparison with Schofield's 1965 data, this shows a fourfold increase in the percentage of adolescent girls who engage in sexual intercourse, while the boys' percentage remained constant. While the percentage of females who had intercourse increased in the decade between 1965 and 1975, certain cultural attitudes remained constant. Many boys and girls still believe that a man has to "conquer" and protect the woman. Some attitudes of the boys seem to have changed towards androgyny, with more boys reporting a desire for a "love relationship" rather than a desire to satisfy an urge.

Schlaegel et al. present one of the few surveys in which the sexual attitudes of preadolescents as young as 11 years were tested. In order to avoid embarrassment these investigators encapsulated their questions in comics so that a subject's attitude could be projected toward a third person. It was found that marked attitude changes occurred between the ages of 11 and 16. For instance, almost all 11-year-olds said they wanted a family, but by the age of 16 only two-thirds had this desire. At age 11 preadolescents believe that sex is for the purpose of propagation, but later they believe that it is part of friendship and love. One of the most drastic opinion changes was reported on the topic of premarital sex. Nearly all 11-year-old boys and girls want to wait with sex until marriage, but by the ages 14–16 almost all reject this type of abstinence. One wonders how much the physiological changes occurring at adolescence are responsible for this attitudinal change. Has physiology got the better of them?

The cited data do not reveal to what degree the observed sexual practices are innate or culturally acquired. If we postulate that it is our culture and education that makes the male more active or aggressive, we should ask ourselves why 80 per cent of the boys between the ages of 11–19 do not engage in intercourse. On the other hand, the finding that girls in 1965 surpassed boys in the frequency of intercourse once they had experienced it suggests that this first act was rewarding enough to lift the culturally imposed inhibition. This may be compared to the results of Bandura's study (see Chapter 4), which showed that girls "learned" to be aggressive but did not act it out until they were socially rewarded. But if we postulate cultural influences, we should also ask why the girl's first sexual contact removed the cultural restriction "not to have sex," but not the restriction of having "one partner only." The desire of having one partner who is loved seems to be as prevalent in the 1970s as it was in the 1960s, although the percentage of girls having intercourse has risen sharply. The attitudes that changed during this decade were those of the boys who in the 1970s tended to consider sex more a matter of friendship (rather than physical satisfaction) than they had in the 1960s.

In Schofield's study male and female adolescents reported several different reactions to sexual intercourse. Most of the boys and half the girls reported that it was enjoyable. There were larger differences as to the frequencies with which climax was experienced. Over half of the boys, but only 14 per cent of the girls answered "always," and hardly any boys, but one quarter of the girls, answered "never." There was also a larger percentage of girls than boys who did not know if they had reached an orgasm or not. The experience of an orgasm seems to be more diffuse and less distinct for girls. Schofield asked boys and girls whether they experienced an orgasm during their first intercourse, and he also asked them to judge if their respective partner experienced an orgasm. The percentage of the boys (80 per cent) who experienced an orgasm was assessed rather correctly by the girls; the girls' percentage (28 per cent) was overestimated by the boys: double to that which the girls reported for themselves. The boys apparently mistook certain behavior for orgasm, or perhaps they were bragging!

Adult Sexuality

Do age and practice develop sexual feelings and actions typical for each sex? Many culturally established sex-role differences have been discussed in the previous chapters; we shall now examine adult sexual behavior with respect to male and female differences and similarities.

There are several physiological actions and reactions that occur, although to different degrees, in both males and females during the sex act. The sex flush, a redness on the stomach surface, occurs shortly before orgasm in 75 per cent of females, but only in 25 per cent of the males. The heartbeat increases on the average in men 170 per cent and in women 130 per cent, and perspiration after orgasm is common in one third of both sexes (Sigusch, 1971). Males need less time and less practice to have an orgasm. Kinsey et al. (1953) found that 90 per cent of the males had experienced an orgasm by the age of 15, while women did not reach this percentage until the age of 29. There are also differences in the reported pathologies. Men complain most frequently about the inability to have an erection, women most frequently about the inability to experience orgasm.

The literature about male orgasm is not as detailed as that written about female orgasm. As already mentioned, the male orgasm is more distinct and of a shorter duration than the female orgasm. It occurs in conjunction with ejaculation, although Matussek (1971) reports of homosexual males who have experienced ejaculation without orgasm during intercourse with females, and there are also reports of males having orgasm without ejaculation. Physiologically the female orgasm consists of between three and fifteen muscular contractions, one second apart, which have been described as being similar to birth pangs. The uterus swells sometimes to double its normal size. Some physiological reactions culminate before the actual orgasm occurs. Breasts, the clitoris, and the labia minor and major show no specific reaction during the orgasm. There is also a dulling of the senses, including the sense of pain, moments during which masochistic actions such as bitings and beatings may not be felt as painful experiences.

Questionnaire methods used with hundreds of women (Kinsey et al., 1953; Fisher, 1973) indicate that excitement during orgasm mounts to a high tension and is followed by a sudden release. This feeling lasts on the average of six to ten seconds; most women report that they have no thoughts, feelings, or images during this interval, although retrospectively they describe the experience most often as ecstatic, happy, and as "if I would burst." The average time for a married and experienced woman to reach an orgasm is eight minutes, with large individual differences ranging from one to thirty minutes.

There has been much speculation about the observed male-female difference in orgasmic experience. Kinsey and his co-workers point out that the woman's delay is caused by an ineffective stimulation by her partner, since during masturbation the length of time by which orgasm can be reached is almost equal for both men and women—ranging from about two to four minutes. It was also found that the percentage of women who experience orgasm increases with the length of time they are married. This would again indicate that there is a practice effect or the loss of an initial cultural inhibition.

Other data suggest innate physiological sex differences with respect to orgasm capacity. Females can have multiple orgasm, one right after another, something males in general cannot do. After orgasm most males find further stimulation of their penis unpleasant and need a rest period before they can have a second or third ejaculation. Those men who can have sequential orgasm report that the first one is the most satisfying, while women who experience multiple orgasm report that the second or third is most satisfying. A further physiological difference is the reaction between age and orgasm capacity. The frequency with which males can have orgasm decreases with age, while the female capacity does not seem to be age dependent. We may postulate a practice effect for females but not for males.

The first sexual experience seems to make less of a lasting impression on males than on females. A man is more inclined to perceive his sexual relations as something separate from himself, as something anatomical or functional. He has more orgasm without a partner, often during sleep without dreams or other psychic involvement. A woman's sexual satisfaction depends more on psychological factors; her genital feelings are more an integral part of her life and her love (or loves), something that Matussek (1971) has termed an "inner preparedness."

Fisher, as reported in his book, *The Female Orgasm* (1973), attempted to investigate this inner preparedness, or what he called the "determinants of orgasm capacity." His sample consisted of several hundred married, middle-class women between the ages of 21 and 45. He found remarkably few factors that one might think would influence a woman's sexual responsiveness. Such factors as age, religion, degree of religiosity, number of pregnancies, and source of education were not related to orgasm consistency. Surprisingly the attributes of a woman's sex partner were also found to be unrelated (within limits) to her orgasm experience. It made no difference whether her partner was happy or how he felt about their relationship. Being an only child and having an education were some of the few factors positively related to orgasm capacity. The opposite should be expected if one has the stereotyped belief that Western education is unnatural and sexually inhibiting; those who have had more formal parental and scholastic education should have fewer and not more orgasm. Yet the "inner dependency" alone does not seem to be a sufficient stimulus for orgasm, which needs an additional physical stimulus in most cases. In Kinsey's survey only 2 per cent of the women reported that they could reach an orgasm through fantasy—which gives romanticism a low score!

The women in Fisher's survey reported that they had intercourse three to four time per week and that they were satisfied with this amount, although the majority of them felt that their husbands would prefer intercourse one more time per week. The average foreplay lasted 12 minutes and the following types of foreplay are ranked in their order of preference: (1) Clitoris; (2) Vagina near clitoris; (3) Inside lips of vulva; (4) Inside vagina; (5) Breasts; and (6) Outside lips of vulva. More than half of the women who did not regularly experience orgasm reported that they enjoyed intercourse in spite of this inconsistency. There were also preferred times in the menstrual cycle, with the highest responsiveness during the week after menstruation and the second highest during the week before.

Intercourse has been described as a "dual masturbation" procedure indicating that it does not make any difference who and in which way the other partner receives his satisfaction (Kroger & Freed, 1950). Fisher's case histories, however, show that much of the woman's satisfaction depends on the stimulation received from her partner and on observing the partner being excited and stimulated. In general, intercourse proceeded as follows: First there is foreplay during which most women are touched and kissed on various body areas such as mouth, lips, breasts, clitoris; then the woman enters into the more active part; next is penile intromission and/or manual stimulation of the clitoris until orgasm is reached. In about one third of the cases orgasm was reached together, the other two thirds divided evenly into experiencing orgasm either earlier or later.

The highpoints of excitation during intercourse are different for females and males. Matussek (1971) has pointed to the functional value of these time differences; while one partner is temporarily less excited the other one experiences more intense feelings. Although this "nontogetherness" may now be considered disturbing, it may have been important for human survival in the past. At least one sex partner could be alert during intercourse and could discern danger from animals and hostile humans.

DISCUSSION

Sex consists of observable physiological reactions and of subjectively experienced feelings. When we study children we can readily observe physiological reactions that occur during erections and genital stimulation, but we have no method of assessing the accompanying feelings. Therefore we cannot state with any assurance that a child's reactions are truly sexual. Some of the distinct attitudinal changes occurring between ages 11 and 16 suggest that the preadolescent reflects a cultural or verbally learned value without being physiologically involved. Feelings of adolescents and adults, however, can be studied because verbal reports can be given and questionnaires can be filled out. If there is a problem in assessing adult sexuality it is the adults' reluctance to perform while physiological data are recorded.

In spite of these difficulties a considerable amount of data obtained in different investigations indicate that females do not experience orgasm as regularly as men. Their sexual feelings vary more between and within individuals and in general they emphasize "love" in single partner relationships.

The existing research leaves us no definite answer as to the degree of the innate or acquired qualities of sex. There are indications that women need to "learn" sexual gratification during months or years of practice. It has been postulated that this learning is necessary because females have been culturally conditioned against sex and sexual pleasures. On the other hand, there was the observation that those females who have more education have fewer inhibitions, which makes one wonder which components of our culture condition sexual inhibition. The mere physiological fact that females can receive gratification through several modes of stimulation may also be responsible for their more varied sexual feelings and for the longer time required to reach orgasm and sexual satisfaction. Physiology and culture are intricately involved, because the flexibility of the partner and the communication between partners will also determine how soon the female's optimal gratification is obtained.

Once a woman has found a satisfactory mode of gratification she may be inclined to keep her partner in order to avoid a new adjustment process, which takes longer in females than in males. While there is much evidence that our culture teaches a woman to be in love and dependent on a single partner, biological factors cannot be ruled out. We must also consider the hypothesis that it may be "natural" for the male to prefer a single partner and that his tendency to change partners is a culturally conditioned phenomenon. Recent changes in the attitudes of male adolescents indicate a shift to the more "feminine" preferences.

The above suggestions are speculative. There is a difference between female and male sex and only a beginning of the physiological and the cultural causes are understood. Freud recognized the female's involvement with two different types of sexual stimulation possibilities, but unfortunately he speculated or perhaps moralized that only the vaginal stimulation was the mature and normal mode of satisfaction. This one-sided approach, which has confused much of the educated public for decades, has been disproved by the knowledge gained through a number of extensive surveys.

Chapter 8

MEASURING MALE-FEMALE DIFFERENCES

Since the turn of the century psychologists have tried to assess male and female traits. As Leona Tyler (1965) points out, those assessments have generally supplied the type of information society wanted. Early in 1900 psychologists tested males and females for various mental abilities and showed that the sexes are equal in their intellectual capacities (see Chapter 5: Education and Intellect). Several decades later, around the 1940s, psychological research aims changed toward investigating male and female differences. In this period society in general and psychologists and sociologists in particular believed that happiness could best be attained by men pursuing the occupations and women the homemaking, in a sort of "compensating togetherness." In the 1970s the psychological tests measuring male and female traits have come under scrutiny since the sex-role, the very dimensions they measure, have been questioned. It is not questioned whether sex-roles exist, but whether and in what way they ought to exist. Almost all the approaches to sex-role equalization suggest the acceptance or rejection of certain sex-role traits for either females or males. Thus it still remains a necessity to define that which is female and that which is male so that certain typically male or female traits can be taught or omitted to be taught in the socialization process. The present chapter will discuss psychological tests by which psychologists attempt to define various dimensions of personality, attitudes, interest, and behaviors with respect to male-female differences.

As mentioned previously there is no difference between the mean IQ score of boys and girls. When the Binet Test was developed around the turn of the century sex differentiating items were deliberately eliminated as the test makers were not interested in defining intelligence so that there would be a difference between the sexes. That scores are equal tells us merely that the sexes are equal in intelligence only as defined and measured by the Binet Scale and similar tests. Test designers can manipulate the presence or absence of sex differences. To a question such as "Do you like coffee?" they will obtain about an equal proportion of "yes" and "no" answers from both females and males, while to a question such as "Do you like boxing?" the response ratio will be unequal with more males than females responding favorably. Thus the items of a test can be selected to indicate either similarities or dissimilarities. This can only be done after a test has been administered and after it has become apparent which items are answered differently by the sexes and which are not. Psychologists have obtained unexpected sex differences on some items designed for character and personality scales. In other instances they did not obtain the differences they expected. Whether intended or not, sex differences have been found in numerous psychological evaluations and assessments. They seem to exist but they are evasive, and it is difficult to fit them into one single "masculine-feminine" dimension.

Vocational Inventories

The most practical definition of masculinity-femininity can perhaps be found in relation to the vocational inventories. For the construction of these tests sex differences were emphasized because they existed in reality in the vocations, and these tests were designed to select personnel for the much sex-stereotyped vocations. This rationale seemed so obvious that Terman & Miles (1936) developed a masculinity-femininity (M-F) scale based entirely on examining and rating a variety of vocations.

In constructing their scale they gave engineers the highest masculine rating, followed by lawyers, teachers, farmers, and police and firemen who were given the lowest masculine rating. Domestic servants were highest on the feminine scale, followed by housewives, nurses, and high school teachers who were assigned the lowest feminine score. Apparently scientific and political abilities were given a higher masculine value than adventure or physical fitness, otherwise one would expect that policemen and firemen would have been rated high on the masculine scale. The definition of that which is masculine (and from a sexist view that which is better) seems to change over the decades. Perhaps scientists were rated more masculine because there were fewer scientists than adventurers. It is also possible that the image of a policeman in the 1930s was closer to the friendly neighborhood cop than to today's shoot-outs and speeding police cars. Much of the definition of masculinity and femininity depends on the culture and its period as well as on the preferences and interests of the test designer.

The Strong Vocational Interest Blank (SVIB) and the Kuder Preference Record have been the most widely used tests to measure vocational interests and to advise prospective candidates which areas to study and which vocations to select. Both tests reflect existing sex-role trends and it was (and perhaps still is) not difficult to predict that males would be vocationally most successful if their interests were in mechanics, science, adventure, business, and politics; and that women would do best if they were inclined toward music, art, literature, social work, and teaching.

The SVIB investigates a person's interest in general and in specific occupations, in academic achievement, and in male and female activities. From these various categories males are given scores (estimates on how well they would do) for 59 occupations and females for 34. The M-F category may enter into a counseling situation in the following way: If a male shows a high engineering interest, but scores low on masculinity, he may be advised to select architecture as an alternative as it may be reasoned that less masculine males are more artistic and creative than the very masculine ones. In this manner vocational interest inventories not only reflect vocational categorization, but also maintain them. As in the above example, engineering is not recommended to feminine males, thereby keeping this profession purely "male."

The SVIB was first published in 1927 and has had a continuous and successful history (Karmel, 1970). Persons who have selected their vocations with its help stayed longer on the job and reported greater satisfaction than persons who selected their careers without it. Employees holding the same job in the same companies for 30 years have been retested and have shown a remarkable stability in their job-related interests. This indicates that attitudes and habits related to the vocations are of long standing and that certain amounts of dissonance and resistance to equal employment practices should be expected.

The Kuder Preference Record (1948) examines interests in outdoor activities, mechanics, computations, science, persuasiveness, literature, music, social science, and clerical activities. It tests these areas for both males and females but provides different profile scales for the sexes.

A male, for instance, performs on the 50th percentile if he scores positive on 46 of the mechanical items, while the female midpoint lies at only 26 positively answered mechanical items. In the social science category, in contrast, the female's midpoint lies at 63 positive items and the male's at 46. Many persons who have followed the recommendations and the sexual dichotomy of the vocational interest inventories have been satisfied for years, particularly the males. For the females it may be different as the labor statistics (see Chapter 6) indicate that females who have not entered the typical categories earn more money than those who have. Female store owners who stock automotive parts, for instance, earn more money than females who stock wearing apparel.

A more recent version of the Kuder Preference Record is the Kuder Occupational Interest Survey (OIS). It provides scores for males for 79 occupations and for females for 56. Over a third of the women's scores were obtained from scales developed with male criterion groups in fields where men dominate but which also offer opportunities to women (Anastasi, 1968). This is an interesting and necessary development, as it leads the vocational interest tests away from the sex-role stereotypy, which they have maintained if not propagated for decades (Birk, 1974). Whether sex-specific interest inventories were historically justified or not, they have helped to guide many females and males into vocations in which they were satisfied. It is quite possible that they will continue to do this without any male-female categorizations.

Personality Tests

Many personality tests emphasized male-female differences because it was part of their purpose to measure the degree to which an individual's responses agree with those characteristic of men or women in our culture (Anastasi, 1968).

One of the most frequently used personality tests is the Minnesota Multiphasic Personality Inventory (MMPI). It attempts to assess such neurotic and psychotic symptoms as depression, hysteria, paranoia, social introversion, and masculinity-femininity. In detail its M-F scale attempts to measure the degree of a person's sexual "inversion," which means the femininity of males and the masculinity of females. These inverted values were thought to permeate many of a person's values, attitudes, and interests. At the extremes they were believed to be linked to sexual inhibitions and psychopathological states. Females who rated high towards femininity, towards the "normal," were described as sensitive, modest, responsive, grateful, and wise. Hence it was considered normal for a female to be sensitive, but not for a male.

Though the M-F scale was designed to reflect the cultural norms of the times, no single scale could do justice to the great variety of human traits and attitudes in which M-F differences appear. There were too many exceptions that the scales predicted in a conflictual way. College males, for instance, received higher femininity scores than noncollege males because they answered certain questionnaire items in a more literary or aesthetic way, although they were by no means feminine in other aspects of their behavior. The *MMPI Handbook* (1972) lists over a dozen different M-F subscales, each one attempting to measure M-F differences in a different human behavioral or attitudinal dimension. The many different scales became necessary when it was found that masculinity and femininity influence different aspects of a person's personality. For example, the same male may be rated as very masculine on a scale measuring "sexuality" and as feminine on a scale measuring "adventure." Not only is there a low correlation between the M-F subscales of the MMPI, but there is also little or no correlation between a person's M-F scores on different tests, such as the Strong Vocational Interest Blank, the MMPI, and the

Guilford Zimmerman Temperament Survey, a test that attempts to measure confidence, sociability, objectivity, and tolerance.

It was the underlying rationale of the MMPI and of many other personality tests that it was to one's own satisfaction and to that of society to function within the culturally accepted sex-roles. The Draw-A-Person test, which was developed by Machover (1949), was based on the same rationale. It found extensive use for testing children's anxieties, conflicts, and compensatory mechanism, claiming that these difficulties can be detected from the way children draw a person. It was believed that children who draw a self-sex figure identify with their own sex and that those who draw opposite sex figures are sexually "inverted." Worse yet, it was held that a maladjusted child will scramble sex cues, drawing pants and earrings, skirt and pipe, etc. Although those hypotheses have seldom been supported by research (Swensen, 1957) the Draw-A-Person test has found continuous use since its first publication.

There are a number of tests specifically designed to test masculinity and femininity, most notably Guilford's Masculinity Scale (1936) and Gough's Femininity Test (1952). As described by Constantinople (1973), Guilford's Masculinity Scale defines somewhat arbitrarily certain masculine activities (e. g., "like to sell things") and certain feminine activities (e. g., "has kept a personal diary"). Persons taking the test indicate which activities pertain to them. The original scale of 36 items was later extended to 123 items and was then thought to be predominantly a measure of dominance and submission. A still later revision resulted in a very heterogeneous masculinity factor being composed of such characteristics as fearfulness, inhibition of emotional interests, distrustfulness, and sympathy. There has been an extensive overlap between the responses of males and females and the question has been raised whether this scale measures more a "masculine ideal" than an actual sex difference.

Gough's Femininity Scale was developed for the purpose of separating "sexual deviates from normals." Males who score high on this scale have been judged psychologically as affectionate, courageous, dependent, gentle, honest, modest, sensitive, and tolerant; while those who scored low were seen as ambitious, cool, dignified, hardheaded, humorless, self-centered, self-confident, tense, and weary. These adjectives seem to describe something like a social awareness as much as femininity and those describing the high scoring males are in general more favorable than those assigned to the low scoring group. With respect to favorability there are some contradictions within the above adjective groups. It is hard to imagine a person with an outstanding trait such as "courageous" who has another outstanding trait labeled "dependent." There are also contradictions within the adjectives describing the low scoring males. Persons who are "cool" and "self-confident" are not likely to be "tense" and "weary."

Contradictory traits have bothered psychologists in all areas of personality assessment. For more than 2,000 years, ever since Aristotle, humans have been thought of as belonging to certain types, such as sanguine (cheerful) and melancholic (gloomy), or perhaps in more modern terms, extraverts and introverts. These classifications were considered as bipolar "types" and as forming a continuum. The same is often assumed to be the case with the masculine-feminine dimension. As psychologists began to study people more intensely they began to form "trait" concepts. While a person could only be of one type, there could be many traits by which he or she could be described. A person could be extroverted, friendly, intelligent, and ambitious all at the same time. As discussed later, the M-F dimension seems to be composed of a number of traits that may or may not be related to each other, even though various tests combine these traits into one final score, giving the impression that M-F is a singular type-characteristic.

The Gough scale has shown how adjectives describing traits can contradict each other. There are also contradictions with type categorizations. There are, for instance, people who are antisocial in the morning hours of the day but who become gregarious toward the evening. Such people have been described as "ambiverts," being both introverts and extraverts. But opposing traits give us little information unless we specify the situation and the instances in which a person is likely to be extraverted or introverted, or in which situations he or she is likely to act feminine or masculine. The issue of opposing traits will again be discussed when we consider androgyny, which suggests that all people, male and female, should be masculine as well as feminine.

Many psychologists who constructed and used personality and diagnostic tests had accepted the Freudian doctrine discussed in the previous chapter, which assumes that a normal adjustment in life depends on the appropriate sex-role development and identification. This doctrine, although still prevalent among psychoanalysts, has lost some of its force since homosexuality has been legalized in many countries and since some people began to wonder if the world would not be a better place if males were less masculine and more feminine in their characteristics. Further contradictions have been found in the relationship between masculinity and positive adjustment for males. Longitudinal data from the Berkeley Growth Study (Mussen, 1962) indicate that males who rate high on masculinity (or low on femininity) show better adjustment in adolescence than males who are more feminine. In later life, however, the more feminine male seems to fare better. He shows more self-acceptance and a lesser need for abasement. Such traditional masculine traits as ambitiousness, determination, confidence, and physical fitness support the cultural expectations of adolescent males, but they do not seem to further the social skills needed by the males in their advancing years. Physical skills, for instance, central to traditional masculinity, decline faster than intellectual or interpersonal ones, thereby causing greater adjustment difficulties for the masculine male at middle or old age. The counterpart, the highly feminine female, does not seem to experience similar adjustment problems.

There are a number of personality tests which were not designed to test sex-role differences, but were found to do so after they were designed. The Maudsley Personality Inventory (MPI), for example, was developed by Eysenck in 1959 to measure the degree of a person's extraversion and introversion as well as neuroticism. Questions that assess extraversion-introversion asked about an individual's vivaciousness, sociability, number of friends, number of parties attended, initiative, etc. Questions that determine neuroticism asked about feelings of loneliness, crisis, weakness, etc. Large sex differences were found in the answers to 29 out of 261 items pertaining to extraversion. Examining these 29 sex-discordant items Eysenck and Eysenck (1969) found that the trait of extraversion has a somewhat different composition for men than it has for women. For men it means being carefree, being in the foreground on social occasions, not being sensitive to criticism, being quick and sure in action, etc. For women extraversion means being impulsive, liking social engagements, being good at bluffing when in difficulty, and starting new jobs with enthusiasm. In general men score more highly on the extraversion scale and women more highly on the introversion scale. When extraverts become neurotic they are likely to be psychopaths and have conduct problems such as fighting and sexual perversion. When introverts become neurotic they tend to have melancholia, guilt feelings, depressions, and feelings of inferiority. Thus Eysenck's scale predicts the higher number of male convicts as well as the higher number of females in psychiatric care.

Androgyny Scales

In the 1970s the idea of normalcy with respect to sex-roles swung toward the middle and away from the two extremes of masculinity and femininity. As described by Sandra Bem (1975, 1976) the notion that masculinity is a necessary mark of the psychologically healthy male and femininity the mark of a healthy female has outlived its usefulness. Many advocates of women's liberation believe that an individual will have a fuller and richer life if he or she is androgynous; that is, by having a repertoire of both feminine and masculine characteristics and by being free to choose from either according to the appropriateness of the situation—something Bem calls a "psychological bisexuality."

In order to assess androgyny in the American society, Sandra Bem (1974) designed the "Bem Sex Role Inventory" (BSRI), which contains 20 items representing such typical female characteristics as affection, gentleness, and understanding, and 20 typical male items which test ambition, dominance, and self-reliance. In this test a person is asked to indicate how well each of these items describes himself or herself. The more male items and the fewer female items a person endorses, the higher will be the masculinity score; conversely, the fewer male items and the more female items the higher the femininity score. The more often a person selects both male and female items the higher will be the androgyny score.

In administering this test to over 1500 male and female undergraduates at Stanford University, Bem found that 27 per cent of the females and 34 per cent of the males scored in the androgynous category. It is interesting that this scale showed that more males than females were androgynous.

From the "IT" scale to be discussed later and from various other tests measuring attitudes about games and vocations, one would expect that more females than males score androgynous because females have more cultural leeway toward accepting the masculine. The larger percentage of males in the androgynous groups may also have been caused by the fact that the men in Bem's sample were college men who, as was shown by the MMPI, are more feminine in some of their responses than are noncollege men.

In 1975 Sandra Bem attempted to validate her scale by trying to find out whether the BSRI would predict actual behaviors typical for both males and females. Both male and female Stanford University students and independent judges had rated "independence" (saying what you believe when you know those around you disagree) as highly masculine and "playfulness" (playing with a six-week-old baby kitten) as highly feminine.

First, Bem obtained sex-role inventory scores from her subjects and then observed each subject's "independence" (yielding to the opinion of others while judging comics) and also each subject's "playfulness" (observing interaction with a baby kitten). Bem found that both male and female subjects who scored high on masculinity and androgyny on her inventory (BSRI) were more independent than those subjects who scored high on femininity. Hence her scale is a valid predictor of the masculine trait of "independence" within the limits of the test situation (not conforming to the opinion of others in rating comics). The playing with the kitten, however—the feminine task—could only be predicted by the BSRI for males, not for females. Males high in masculinity and androgyny on the BSRI played much less with the kitten than males high on femininity, but contrary to expectations, females high on masculinity played more often and more intensely with the kitten than females high on femininity—which is contrary to what the BSRI is trying to predict.

Sandra Bem discusses this unexpected result and suggests that the females have "flunked" the test, that feminine females have the "most serious behavioral deficit," and that femininity in females is generally associated with high anxiety and poor social adjustment. If such factors should prevent the expression of femininity involving a kitten, one may wonder why they do not prevent the expression of femininity while answering items in a sex-role inventory. But it has been frequently found that there are differences between verbal reports and actual behavior. We may further wonder why it is suggested that feminine females have a serious deficit because they do not play with kittens when no such suggestions are made for those masculine males who did play with them. Kitten playing may be composed of the female "caring and nurturing" and of the more male actions of "animal handling." Feminine females may predominantly consider this latter aspect of the kitten playing situation—thus behaving quite normal with respect to the culturally accepted sex-role behavior.

To investigate the caring for infants, Bem (1976) observed how college students interacted with a six-month-old baby for a 10-minute period. As expected only few masculine males (21 per cent) interacted with the infant as compared to 50 per cent of the androgynous males. Among the female students, however, there was no such differentiation. The androgynous as well as the feminine females interacted with the infant in the same proportions: 50 per cent in both groups. From the conventional notion of femininity, one would have expected a higher percentage among the feminine females than among the androgynous ones.

In another attempt to validate her androgyny scale (BSRI), Bem measured the empathy that students displayed while interacting with persons who pretended they had psychological problems. With the amounts of listening, nodding, and verbally expressed concern as measures of empathy, it was found that only few masculine males (14 per cent) exhibited it. A much higher percentage (60 per cent) of the androgynous males and females showed empathy, and the feminine females were reported to react strongest by showing more interest for the problems of others than androgynous females.

Bem believes that in the future androgyny will constitute a new basis for psychological health because it gives us the possibilities to be both independent and gentle, self-assured and self-denying, masculine and feminine, etc.

The desirability as well as the feasibility of androgyny, however, should be seriously questioned. While it may give an individual a chance to react one way or the other it may restrict the range of human reactions. In a completely androgynous society, for example, the masculine male group, in which only 14 per cent showed empathy, would not exist; neither would the feminine female group, which showed the highest degree of understanding. It is further questionable if an androgynous person will have a freer choice in her or his own reactions. A male who is androgynous can be independent in not letting his opinion be influenced by others. He can also be gentle and play with a kitten. But would an androgynous male also have the choice not to maintain his own opinion, and not to play with a kitten?

Many of the definitions of androgyny have not been worked out, as Bem's own validation procedures have shown. Her work, however, has shown that the conventional concepts that our society has about masculinity and especially about femininity fitted the majority of opinions, but they did not stand up under empirical tests. While there is agreement in our beliefs that feminine females play with kittens and babies, the actual observations have shown that these behaviors are not particularly related to femininity. The incongruence of a generally expressed opinion and an actually observed behavior has bothered psychologists since their discipline began (Schmidt, 1976). The most sophisticated tests and statistical procedures are of doubtful value if they are merely based on beliefs, ideas, attitudes, or opinions. In this respect, Bem's work about androgyny is very promising because besides opinions she also investigates the actual behavior of her subjects.

Toy Preference Tests and Children's Scales

Maleness and femaleness have always been among the major attributes by which we judge children. While certain of the "observed" differences between the behaviors of male and female infants are in the mind of the observer (see Chapter 3), there are many boy and girl differences that have become a reality by the age of two. Whether caused by the child's actions and/or by our own stereotyped reactions, children as well as adults conceptualize male-female categories, which they then use as norms when observing and describing children. Proximity to the parent, the child's general activity, and more specifically the type of toys and games selected have all been used to assess femininity and masculinity in children.

Brown's "IT" scale for children (ITSC) (1956) was one of the first empirical attempts to measure masculinity and femininity of children between the ages of five and six. In this test the child is shown a drawing of a presumably sexless stick figure and is given a choice of pictured toys that are definitely sex-typed, such as a locomotive or a doll. The child is then asked to pick out the toy appropriate for the "IT" figure from a mixture of feminine and masculine toys. The more masculine toys the child selects, the higher the masculinity score; conversely, the more female toys the higher the feminity score. It was hypothesized that a child would be freer to select a toy for the "IT" figure than for her or his own self, especially if there may be the possibility of shame or nonapproval.

The "IT" scale has several drawbacks. One of its major difficulties is its very projective nature; many children, especially American girls, imagine that the "IT" figure represents a boy and select toys appropriate for boys but do not project their own desire into the situation. (Wanting to be subtle and sophisticated, psychologists often get caught in their own games!) Some studies have shown that children change their choices when the "IT" figure is actually labeled "boy" or "girl" or when it is given the name of the child being tested (Thompson & McCandless, 1970).

To correct the error resulting from a child not identifying correctly with the "IT" figure, De Lucia (1963) designed a Toy Preference Test (TPT) in which an actual drawing of a boy is presented when a boy is tested and a drawing of a girl when a girl is being tested. When tested in that manner each child is shown a sequence of pairs of photographs, each pair picturing one typical feminine toy and one typical masculine toy. Each time a pair of pictures is shown the child being tested is asked with which toy the child in the picture would like to play.

An interesting test battery to measure sex-role attitudes has been developed in Sweden by Wiechel (1972). One of its subtests consists of pictures in which two pairs of hands are shown performing different but related tasks. For example, one pair of hands is shown picking apples, the other pair holding the basket. For each pair of hands the subjects are asked to indicate whether they belong to a girl or a boy. This test attempts to assess specific functions within work areas such as housework, gardenwork, and child care. Carol Anne Dwyer (1974) developed two tests for the grade-school level: the "Sex Role Standard" checklist inquiring about the interests of boys and girls in general, and the "Individual Sex Role Preference" test asking about the respondent's own interests. She found different predictive values for these two tests. Some pupils who showed sex-role stereotypy on one scale did not show it on the other.

Several scales designed to measure anxiety in children find that girls have higher anxiety scores than boys, although they are more sociable than boys and less aggressive (Children's Manifest Anxiety Scale, General Anxiety Scale for Children). Measured with the Junior Eysenck Personality Inventory (1970), boys were found to be more extraverted than girls by the age of seven and this difference remained constant until age fifteen. At seven, girls have a somewhat higher neuroticism score, and this difference keeps on increasing until adolescence. Thus the more frequent neuroticism in women and the more pronounced extraversion in men seem to have their beginnings in childhood. As previously mentioned in the extremes, introversion can lead to mental institutions and extraversion to jails. There are about one quarter more females than males under psychiatric care and, depending on the country, about ten to forty times as many men as women are incarcerated in prisons.

Definition Scales

A number of questionnaire methods have been designed to find out which in general are feminine and which are masculine traits. Before we can assess a person's femininity, masculinity, or androgyny we must first examine the constellation of psychological traits our culture attributes to men, to women, or to both. As Leona Tyler (1965) mentioned, most of our scales that attempt to investigate male-female characteristics have been designed more with differences than with similarities in mind. For example, Rosenkrantz et al. (1968) developed their Sex Role Stereotype Questionnaire (SRSQ) by asking college students to list behaviors, attributes, and characteristics that they thought differentiated men and women, and the Personal

Attribute Questionnaire (PAQ) designed by Spence et al. (1974) was developed under the same principle.

One assessment method based on similarities as well as on differences was developed by Williams and Bennett (1975). They used a 300-word adjective checklist (ACL) originally designed by Gough and Heilbrun (1965) to describe people in general. Williams and Bennett asked college students to indicate whether they associate an adjective more frequently with women or with men, or whether they cannot classify it. A surprisingly large number of adjectives, 272 of the 300, were classified by the average rater. But using a criterion of 75 per cent rater agreement, there were only 33 adjectives that were associated with men and 30 that were associated with women. Because these adjectives were selected by such a high percentage of both males and females, Williams and Bennett termed them "focused" or "primary" stereotypes. Some of the adjectives that were rated by about 90 per cent of the male and female raters as masculine were: adventurous, aggressive, coarse, confident, forceful, independent, stern, strong, tough, and unemotional. Some of the adjectives judged by almost 90 per cent of male and female raters as feminine were: affectionate, emotional, fickle, flirtatious, fussy, nagging, prudish, sentimental, submissive, and whiny.

From the above examples one can readily see that there are many more "positive" or "favorable" adjectives among those associated with masculinity. In the complete list of 33 male adjectives there were 10 positive and 5 negative ones, while among the 30 female adjectives there were only 5 positive but 10 negative ones. These evaluative classifications were obtained by Gough and Heilbrun in 1965 independent of any sex-role or stereotype investigations.

The characteristics shown in the above examples are congruent with the general sex stereotypes. The complete lists of male and female adjectives, however, contained a few "surprises." The authors state that they would not have expected that the adjectives coarse, disorderly, jolly, and severe would have been considered so highly masculine, nor that the adjectives appreciative, complaining, and sophisticated would have been considered so highly feminine. Although the total male list of the primary stereotypes contain more positive adjectives than the total female list, there are some evaluative contradictions within the male and female categories; for example, coarse and jolly on the male list and appreciative and complaining on the female list.

Williams and Bennett expanded their male and female lists and included adjectives that had been categorized as male or female by fewer than 75 per cent and by more than 60 per cent of the raters. When they examined these added or "secondary" adjectives they found an interesting shift in the evaluative classification. There were many more favorable adjectives such as cheerful, conscientious, considerate, forgiving, friendly, and kind associated with females rather than with males. The associations made with males such as arrogant, cynical, egotistical, greedy, impatient, and hostile were in the majority unfavorable. The favorability of the two sex stereotypes seems to depend on the degree of penetration into the stereotypes. The female favorability appears to be more subtle. This finding may be related to certain contradictions and frustrations people experience when they evaluate sex-role stereotypy. On "first thought" our stereotypes are decidedly positive on the male side, on "second thought," however, if we consider the more subtle characteristics, we find the favorableness on the female side.

Critique

A number of critical reviews have appeared in the recent literature pointing to various shortcomings under which the concept of masculinity-femininity has been developed and tested. Pleck (1975) mentions the multidimensionality of the M-F as a major drawback. The M-F includes such different components as emotional qualities, interests, and abilities having little empirical relationship with each other. This is the reason why certain M-F scales do not correlate with each other—one scale putting an emphasis on emotions, another on interests, etc. Instead of trying to give individuals one composite score, it would be more informative to work with an M-F profile giving one score for emotionality, one for vocational interests, one for dominance-submission, etc.

Pleck also mentions that M-F scales have been purposely designed to measure differences. He calls attention to the fact that the M-F differences constitute a relatively small proportion of the personality domain. While it is useful to keep this point in mind it should also be pointed out that sex-differences have been found in personality tests that did not intend to measure them, such as the Maudsley Personality Inventory and the Adjective Check List discussed previously. From 300 adjectives examined by Williams and Bennett (1975), 30 were definitely associated with maleness and 30 with femaleness, and an additional number were associated with the sexes to a less definite degree. Thus about one third of a list of 300 adjectives originally not composed to measure sex-differences did indicate them. This very broad spectrum in which sex-role differences appear does suggest their existence.

Anne Constantinople (1973) has presented a very extensive review of the M-F concept and its tests. She believes that it is the "muddiest" concept in the psychologist's vocabulary. It is her main criticism that it is not a single dimension and that anything that discriminates at a particular point in time in a particular culture has been taken as an indicator of M-F. She further believes that these indicators do not relate to other traits or behaviors of the individual. More specifically, Constantinople points to the confusion of how M-F relates to such terms as sex-role identity, sex-role preference, and sex-role adoption.

Sex-role preference can be distinguished from sex-role adoption on the basis of activities one would prefer to engage in as contrasted to those one actually does. The present authors found this distinction of utmost importance when replicating Williams and Bennett's Adjective Check List study at a German university. About half the students refused to fill out the questionnaire after reading the instructions: "Mark those adjectives with an X that are more frequently associated with masculinity than with femininity." Before proceeding they wanted to know whether these instructions meant "what they" or "what people in general" associate. This distinction, or perhaps this conflict, has been pointed out in the discussion of children's scales with children who respond very differently to the questions "what do you like?" and "what do other children like?"

The term "sex-role identity" is even more difficult to define and to measure than sex-role preference or sex-role adoption. It has been used to indicate wishful as well as realistic sex-role performance and sex-role adoption. A homosexual male, for example, has certain female preferences as well as adoptions, yet he may identify himself as a male.

Constantinople believes that most M-F tests assume unidimensionality and bipolarity although there is enough evidence that separate masculinity and femininity dimensions exist, possibly in addition to a bipolar dimension. The assumption of bipolarity would mean a man low on the masculinity scale is equal to a woman low on femininity. Dominance-submission may serve as an example. If dominance-submission is unidimensional and bipolar, then a nondominant male should be equal to a nonsubmissive woman, both should meet at the middle of the scale at the zero point (Figure A).

	100%		0%		100%
	!	*Male*	!	*Female*	!
Males:	very dom.		not dom.		
Females:			not subm.		very sub.

Figure A   Dominance-submission model with assumed bipolarity.

Working and not-working may serve as an example for a nonbipolar dimension. If we assume in the traditional sense full-time work at the male end and zero work at the female end of the distribution, then 50 per cent or part-time work would be at the middle of this scale. If this scale were bipolar, then as far as work is concerned, a part-time working man ought to be equal to a part-time woman worker. This is not the case because few men work part-time, but for women it is much more usual and therefore one should not expect that a woman working part-time is as masculine as a part-time working man is feminine. Lipman-Blumen (1972) has suggested the concept of "sex-role ideology" in connection with female career goals. Women who want careers, she suggests, have a liberal view of the female role as compared to women who have a traditional view who do not desire careers. A liberal woman, however, may be just as feminine as a traditional one—perhaps even more so if we may include a certain *joi de vivre* in our definition of femininity.

Nonbipolarity has been clearly demonstrated by the kitten-playing behavior tested by Sandra Bem. While kitten playing differentiates on the male scale, it does so in a reverse way on the female side of the scale. The very masculine males did not play with the kittens, but neither did the very feminine females. At the feminine end of the scale, where it should have been 100 per cent, it was practically zero (see Figure B).

Kitten playing		0%		50%		100%
		!	Male	!	Female	!
Males,	expected	none		some		
Males,	observed	none		some		
Females, expected				some		much
Females, observed				much		some

Figure B   Model of nonbipolar kitten playing

There are other dimensions in which the M and F sides of a scale may be totally unrelated. Football and chess may differentiate between high and low masculine males, but these variables will not discriminate on the female side, because females in general play neither football nor chess. An activity may not differentiate among one sex group because few of its members engage in it. An activity may likewise not differentiate if all members do it. When Bem tested the interactions with a six-month-old baby she found that almost all females interacted to about equal degrees— no matter whether they were judged or considered androgynous, somewhat feminine, or very feminine by other tests or scales. Constantinople mentions a hypothetical example of a trait differentiating between, but not within, the sexes. In all probability, she states, the length of the big toe would discriminate men from women, but would not differentiate one woman from another with respect to femininity. A woman with a longer toe would not be less feminine than a woman with a shorter toe. Neither would one expect any correlation between masculinity and the length of a man's toe. Hundreds of years ago the Chinese may have had a very definite notion regarding the correlation between femininity and small feet or toes. This emphasizes the dependency of M-F tests, scales, and values on the culture and subculture in which it is assessed. As Pleck states, the concept of M-F as a psychological trait makes sense in a culture with universal and unchanging sex-role norms, but in our culture with changing norms and social class shifts, M-F designations should be regarded with caution.

DISCUSSION

Tests help us to determine in which areas and to what degree sex-differences exist. The tests themselves, however, do not determine their subject matter. As the discussion on the construction of the IQ and various personality tests has shown, they can be designed to measure similarities as well as differences. Whether a test will demonstrate sex differences or not will greatly depend on the type of capacities, traits, or attitudes it attempts to assess and on the specific items it uses.

The purpose of psychological tests examining femininity and masculinity has changed over the decades. Early in this century they were designed to test areas of similarity, at mid-century they emphasized differences, and in the latter part of this century the test makers are again concerned about similarities. In the 1940s, as was pointed out, Helen Machover, who designed the Draw-A-Person test, believed that the person who draws a figure with both male and female characteristics is maladjusted and unstable. In the 1970s, Sandra Bem, who designed the Bem Sex Role Inventory, believes that a person with both male and female characteristics is well adjusted and very stable.

The usefulness of a test is also determined by technological advances. After the invention of machines, muscular strength has become unimportant and it is of little use to measure its differences. Nor may it be necessary to measure differences in arithmetical speed when pocket calculators will be available for everybody. We should further note that neither the tests nor the differences which they discover prescribe the subsequent social action. Test results that show, for example, that boys are more extraverted than girls can be used to initiate equalization. They can also be used as a rationale for maintaining the status quo recommending that males work in certain jobs and women in others.

Most critical reviews point to the M-F's dependency on a particular culture at a particular time. In a changing culture some sex-role attitudes may disappear a decade or so after a test was developed and standardized, while others show a remarkable constancy. The desire for the first-born child to be a male, for example, has remained constant for decades in diverse cultures. Another point of critique has been the multidimensionality of the M-F traits. The tests measure quantitative as well as qualitative differences, and their results can hardly be expressed in a single M-F score. This broad diversification or the spread of sex-roles into many human traits and interests has made their recognition and definition very elusive. Some critics maintain that it is a fallacy to assume that M-F differences exist. On the other hand, it may be just as fallacious to assume that they do not exist just because psychologists have been unable to define and to measure them successfully.

Chapter 9

TRENDS AND PROSPECTS

In the beginning chapter of this text we discussed different approaches toward the equality of the sexes, and in subsequent chapters we enumerated various stereotypes and inequalities in social relations, work, and education. In this final chapter we shall examine the changes that have occurred in sex-role sterotypy during the last decades and attempt to evaluate the various approaches with respect to their usefulness in bringing about sex-role equality.

Masculinization

The masculinization of women has been the most widely advocated and practiced approach towards equalization. In many ways women are becoming more masculine, notably in their education, which is approaching the men's level. In the United States the percentage of female high school graduates in 1974 (46 per cent) is approaching the male's percentage (49 per cent). The number of female college graduates (500,000 in 1975) doubled during the previous decade. Almost half of all B.A. and M.A. degrees are earned by women. Although women received only 14 per cent of all Ph.D.'s awarded in 1971, that number is expected to rise drastically because the pool of B.A. and M.A. graduates is increasing. The most drastic increase in female education has occurred with the group 25 years and older who do not abandon their educational plans upon marriage or child rearing. The college enrollment for this age group rose from about half a million in 1970 to almost one million in 1974 (Van Dusen et al., 1976).

Despite the increasing education that women obtain, there has been a small but constant decrease in the salary they earn in relation to males. In 1956 females earned 37 per cent less than males, in 1974 they earned 43 per cent less. Several factors may be responsible for this decrease. Much of the female's increased education has been in such typical female areas as nursing and primary education and not in the typical male or technological areas. In the decade from 1964 to 1974 the percentage of women in nursing only declined 1 per cent, from 99 per cent to 98 per cent. Declines in elementary teaching from 88 per cent to 84 per cent and in library work from 87 per cent to 82 per cent were also minimal. On the other hand, the increased participation of women in the typical male professions has been small. In technical drafting this increase has been from 5 per cent to 8 per cent and in designing and accounting from 18 per cent to 24 per cent. The largest professional gains are reported for psychology, where the percentage of women increased from 23 per cent to 41 per cent during the decade (*U.S. News & World Report,* 1975).

Another factor contributing to the female-male pay gap is the increased participation of women in the labor force. In the United States five million more women than men have joined the labor force in the last two decades, and since women have in general less education than men, it would mean that the female labor force as a whole has become educationally more deflated. That may explain the increasing pay gap. It has also been pointed out by Lyle and Ross (1973) that much of our industrial expansion occurred in traditionally low-paying, female jobs requiring manual dexterity, such as soldering and the assembly of electronic parts.

Masculinization has also been reported with regard to attitudes towards vocations. Shephard and Hess (1975) have examined such attitudes in four different age groups by presenting kindergarten children, eighth graders, college undergraduates, and adults with a list of 44 occupations and activities. They asked their subjects to indicate for each item whether the role should properly be undertaken by a male, a female, or by either one. In all age groups except in the kindergarten group females were more liberal, being more willing to have both sexes perform a large number of such traditionally masculine activities as plane flying, fishing, school principalship, horse racing, banking, and owning a factory. Females were also more willing to have both sexes perform such traditionally female activities as ironing, laundering, vacuuming, nursing, and cooking.

Changes in attitudes do not necessarily precipitate changes in actual behavior. To increase the chances of equal education and equal employment, it would almost seem necessary to make such subjects as mathematics, physics, and chemistry high-school requirements. This would give the females who are inclined to avoid these subjects in an elective system a more equal chance to participate in further technological training and work—something that may be very much needed to close the pay gap between females and males. It has also been shown (see Chapter 6) that this pay gap is not necessarily closed by an advancement in the education of females. Litigations that make use of local, state, and federal fair-employment laws may become necessary. Women may have to form separate unions to increase their bargaining power, as Andruesue Gomez did in founding the 150-member Coalition of Women Truck Drivers in Los Angeles.

Further masculinization has occurred in the increasing number of female "heads of households." In the United States one in eight families (7.2 million in 1975) is headed by a woman. This status, however, seems to have certain disadvantages; the female head of household group has less education, less money, and more children than the household groups headed by males.

A negative aspect that has been related to the masculinization of women is the increase in the female crime rate. FBI statistics report an 18 per cent increase for the year 1974 and a 300 per cent increase for both robberies and embezzlement for the years 1960 to 1975. While arrests of females increased 9 per cent in the year 1974, the arrests of males increased only 2 per cent during the same period. However, it is by no means clear that the increase in female criminality has been caused by an increase in masculinization. Chris Rasche (1976) interviewed women prisoners at the Duval County prison farm in Florida and reports that most women prisoners have very traditional desires of staying home and taking care of children and that they do not understand the feminist movement. They consider it as a threat when they are encouraged to go to work. The increased feminine criminality could be caused by factors not related to change in sex-role patterns, such factors as an increased availability in drugs, guns, unemployment, and inflation.

It is tempting to infer causal relationships between sociological changes and the efforts made by certain groups advocating them. A great deal of masculinization, for example, has occurred in the attitudes and in the practices concerning children's play and games before the efforts of the female liberation groups gained impetus in the early 1960s. In 1960 Rosenberg and Sutton Smith examined the play

activities of grade-school children in a similar way to those
employed by Terman (1926) and Lehman and Witty (1927)
30 years earlier. Of 27 activities considered masculine in
the 1920s, only 8 had remained in this category; 17 had
changed to neutral (such as baseball, soccer, and camping);
and two (snap the whip, leap frog) had become feminine by
the 1960s. Of the 23 games played predominantly by girls,
19 were still preferred by girls 30 years later. This is a
definite trend in masculinization because the females have
increased their preference for what were formerly male
activities. Their choices have become widened while the
choices of the males have narrowed. For some reason,
these changes have occurred without reform efforts of certain groups and without specific changes in the reading
material or educational objectives.

The masculinization effort has had only a limited success. At best it has caused changes in attitudes but only
token changes in the traditionally male professions. The
number of women firemen, pilots, school principals, and
factory owners is still minimal in all Western countries. It
should be a further concern for those who advocate masculinization that its success is greatly dependent on economic
growth. Had the economic growth and the increase in
female hirings (17 million as compared to 12 million males
in the last two decades) continued, equality in the number
of male and female workers would have been reached by
the end of the century (*U.S. News & World Report,* 1975).
Under zero economic growth and with an expected decrease in labor and employment due to an increase in
mechanization, a balanced work force may not be reached
by the end of the century. Even if we assume the availability
of female skills in all vocations and a strict adherence to
equal employment practices, vacancies for females would
only occur after males retire or die.

An examination of the trends in masculinization suggests further caution. As Simone de Beauvoir (1976) points

out, women may obtain certain "male" privileges while not getting rid of their "female" duties. She cites the conditions in socialist countries, notably the Soviet Union, where women are economically independent with an equal opportunity for respectable and interesting vocations, but where in addition to their jobs they have to stand in line for groceries for their husbands and children and do generally most of the housework. Beauvoir believes that women in socialist countries as compared to capitalist ones are more respected but also much more tired.

The voting rights women attained half a century ago may serve as an other example. Even though women have voted with about the same turnout as men, they have also voted in the same proportion as men for both candidates and issues, be it for a president or for a war. For decades women voters have preferred men to women in authoritative positions. As recently as the early 1970s only 17 per cent of women in the United States indicated they would rather vote for a woman than for a man as U.S. president (Harris, 1971).

The psychological consequences of masculinization are difficult to assess. Aggression and competition are undesirable traits in males and particularly so if they are used for exclusionist practices against women. Perhaps these traits would become less disturbing if they were also practiced by the female half of the population. On the other hand, it is questionable whether aggressiveness and competitiveness as a whole will be useful in a society where human survival may depend on reducing production and consumption.

The Feminization of Males

Opposite to masculinization is the concept that males should become more feminine so that sex-role equality can be reached. This would require males to become psychologically more intimate, emotional, and dependent. It would also mean that they engage more often in child care and household work and in the "female" professions of nursing and elementary school teaching.

A survey at an Ivy League college by Mirra Komarovsky (1973) has shown that only 7 per cent of the males are of the "feminine" type willing to modify their own career if it should conflict with the career of their wives. Many other studies report likewise little progress in the feminization of males. Infant care and household work are still unpopular with males, attitudinally as well as behaviorally. They have also become more unpopular with women. A survey taken by McCall's magazine (1976) found that the relentless repetition of housework was listed by 31 per cent of its readers as the most frequent source of dissatisfaction —ahead of financial and social concerns—despite the fact that the respondents had recourse to sophisticated appliances. Yet about a third of the respondents in the same study expressed their anger at the women's movement for downgrading the role of the housewife and mother.

If infant care and housework were adequately paid they may be as satisfying as many other types of work. Helge Pross (1975) reports, for example, that German housewives in the upper socioeconomic classes with less than three children find their housework much more satisfying than those in the lower economic classes with more than three children. In the same vein the West German minister for family affairs, Katharina Focke (1975) accuses sociologists of not having emphasized the importance and the dignity of housework. Because they stressed the "no pay" factor they gave the impression that housework is intrinsically bad and degrading. At any event, the downgrading of housework has not been very supportive of the women who have to do it or may like to do it; nor has it been conducive to males to partake in it.

Historically, housework did not always have a bad image. In a follow-up study of genius, Terman & Oden (1959) found that housewives with IQ's around 150 appeared just as satisfied as women in the vocations and professions who were in an equally high IQ range. Instead of pointing to their vocations, the housewives mentioned their families as the source of satisfaction. The argument that housework is unbearable did not fit the most highly intelligent group ever studied. Investigating happiness and its relation to full-time housework, Spreitzer et al. (1975) found that almost as many well educated women (40 per cent) as less educated ones (43 per cent) reported a high degree of happiness while engaged in full-time housework. In the same study about 70 per cent of the full-time homemakers reported marital happiness independent of the years of their formal education. Perhaps these more positive aspects of homemaking will encourage more males to take a try at it!

Certain feminization trends have been reported with retired men who are married to younger and employed women. Ballweg (1967) describes some retired men preparing breakfast for their working wives, doing the laundry, and other household chores. Some degree of feminization has also occurred in elementary education and day care. Male personnel in day-care centers has been increasing, ironically often with the rationale that children need a "male image" to compensate for the increasing number of fatherless homes. Males have also made some inroads in a few "female" occupations. A small number of them have become telephone operators and airplane stewards. A number of popular books (see Chapter 1) have been published to further feminization and to give encouragement and advice to fathers for their interaction with their children. Jack Nichols's book *Men's Liberation: A New Definition of Masculinity*, (1975) enumerates the advantages for males who begin to question the inevitability of aggression and domination. He foresees a saner society when man gives up worship of the intellect, the idolization of competition, the admiration of what is big, and the resort to violence.

Although Nichols gives few specific instructions on how to reach this blissful stage, he envisions the feminized male as being more sharing, gentle, and caring, and as having more time and inclination to interact with his children. He hopes that the father's role in the family will change from the mere "financial functionary" to a cultivated and "easy going" friendship. It is interesting to note that the nuclear family, which is often considered as having the most rigidly delineated sex-roles, is also the one that necessitates male sex-role reversals during sickness and emergencies, when the male cares for the children and prepares the food. As Betty Yorburg (1974) points out, in extended, polygamous, or polyandrous families same-sex substitutes are readily available to take over the activities of a wife or husband who is incapacitated.

It is part of the purpose of feminization to conduce males to partake in household duties and family care. This would give women more freedom, particularly those who live in a nuclear family. In this respect the masculinization and feminization trends are at odds, since several feminist writers advocate the complete eradication of the nuclear family (Kate Millett, 1971) and the refraining from childbearing and housework (Simone de Beauvoir, 1976). However, the feminization of males may benefit the males themselves as it may further the survival of our species. Nichols (1975) concludes that the masculine values have outlived their usefulness in a nuclear age and believes that these values are downright dangerous.

A more immediate advantage of feminization may lie in solving the conflict between the Christian work ethic and its consequent overproduction, which Western countries are beginning to experience. The invention of machines has freed people from work, but not from the philosophy that considers work a virtue. Only five people are now needed to produce as much food as it took 100 people to produce a century ago. There are similar overproductions in many of the other essential and nonessential products and services. Many resources are wasted in these overproductions and again in the advertising intended to "create" a need for the not needed products. Over 1,000 Swedish manufacturers, who employ about 250,000 workers, have applied to their government for subsidies to manufacture goods for stockpile purposes because they cannot be sold. Economists have estimated that the future average workweek in the United States will be about 15 hours with production remaining at its present level. Jobs are bound to decrease and employment will be spread out among more people—including women (Yorburg, 1974). If all these predictions come true, feminization as a philosophy and behavior may best prepare the male for our economic future.

Androgyny

If masculinization would create a world too active and feminization a world too passive—then androgyny, it appears, would be the best of both worlds. As mentioned before, psychologists have suggested that individuals are both feminine and masculine, something that may be termed "individual androgyny." It would mean that each man as well as each woman can be aggressive and also submissive, daring and also cautious, dependent and also independent, etc., and that each can select from these opposite traits "what is most effective at the moment" (Bem, 1975).

Some of the difficulties of defining androgyny and of teaching and practicing it have been discussed in the previous chapter. It should further be mentioned that the teaching of androgyny would require discrimination learning because an individual would have to learn at which moments or in which situations to be aggressive and at which to be submissive, or when to be daring and when to be cautious, etc. Discrimination is more difficult to establish than generalization (see Chapter 4), especially when the situations that require different actions are similar. If the situations in which it is better to act feminine and those in which it is better to act masculine are not clearly differentiated, a middle-of-the-road personality may develop. Instead of fighting in certain instances and running away in others, an individual may simply stand still in all instances.

Individual androgyny would require that both females and males be aggressive in the same situations and be submissive in the same situations; otherwise, sex-role behavior may again precipitate. This would necessitate a more-or-less definite reaction pattern for all individuals, and in the final analysis they would not be freer in their actions than they are in the present sex-stereotyped society. For example, in an ideal androgynous society, both girls and boys would play with dolls as well as with trains. Would a member of either sex be free to play only with dolls or only with trains? If psychologists were successful in establishing individual androgyny, they would equalize all people with respect to femininity and masculinity. Should they also be successful in equalizing the IQ and perhaps introversion and extraversion differences, they may eventually create individuals who are all alike—doing Huxley's Brave New World one better!

A concept of androgyny that has not received much attention could be termed "group androgyny," which suggests that male and female traits be found in a group of males and females, but not necessarily in one and the same individual. It would mean that there are feminine women as well as masculine women and also that there are both masculine and feminine males. The group rather than the individual would be androgynous. This type of androgyny would be simpler to establish, as it would avoid more or less the training of opposite traits to one and same individual. Individual differences would also be maintained and one could still meet some men and some women who would never touch a kitten and some who would touch one on every occasion. We may speculate that group androgyny would eliminate sex-role prejudice because the chances of meeting an aggressive or a submissive woman would be equal and the chances of meeting an aggressive man or woman would also be equal. Group androgyny may dispel prejudice while maintaining individual differences.

It is difficult to assess the androgynous trends that have occurred in the last decades. Unisex in terms of clothing, most notably practiced in China, may be considered a form of androgyny if one views the looseness of the apparel as feminine and the trousers as masculine. It may also be judged as a masculinization if one perceives it primarily as wearing a uniform and as the wearing of pants. The unisex look in Western societies also seems to suggest more masculinization than androgyny. It is interesting to speculate whether the long hair worn by males exhibits a feminization or a masculinization since it is often accompanied by a beard. It could also be defined as androgynous because it manifests something female as well as male.

Some androgynous trends have been reported in spite of the difficulties we encounter in defining and listing the traits necessary for androgyny. The West German *hausfrau,* for instance, no longer depends on her husband to make financial decisions. In every second marriage, finances are a matter of mutual agreement; in every third marriage, they are decided by the wife alone. Some couples change back and forth, but in only 4 per cent of the marriages does the husband have the sole control of the bank account. Thus there is a great deal of androgyny and a good amount of masculinization in the control of money matters among married couples (Helge Pross, 1975).

Trends of androgyny are occurring in our sexual behavior. In a survey conducted by *Redbook* magazine (Robert Levin & Amy Levin, 1975) 100,000 women respondents indicated that the initiation of intercourse and methods of satisfaction are becoming more mutual. About 90 per cent of the respondents reported experiences with oral-genital sex, both giving and receiving it. This is about twice the percentage reported by Kinsey et al. 20 years earlier. Regarding their general sexual activities, 78 per cent of the women described themselves as being always or usually active; six out of ten wives reported that they take the initiative about half of the time. Though the *Redbook* study was based on questionnaires—and for obvious reasons not on observation—it shows a definite change in attitude when compared to the Kinsey data, which were also nonobservational.

Political Trends

In 1975—the official International Women's Year—speculations, research, and some changes relating to sex-role equalization were reported from many countries in the world. Sex-role stereotypy is established through religion, education, and economics, all of which in turn are influenced by politics. Yet sex-role equality is not necessarily bound to any political system as it now exists. Marxism, which has most strongly emphasized the equality of women, has in its daily practice tolerated many inequalities. On the other hand, progress has been made in capitalist countries which have recognized women's rights bit by bit over the last decades.

The liberation of women is not necessarily linked to a particular political philosophy, since Marxist as well as capitalist countries vary among themselves in the degree and in the modes of emancipation they offer. The various laws governing abortion in socialist countries may serve as an example. The abortion laws are very liberal in East Germany, Hungary, and the Soviet Union, with the decision left entirely to the discretion of the woman during the first

12 weeks of pregnancy. The Soviet Union legalized abortions at the time of the revolution, prohibited them in 1936, and made them legal again in 1969. Women's rights were apparently secondary to concerns about labor shortages and birth-rate recessions. Poland also has a liberalized abortion law, but certain political factions attempt to limit this law from time to time. In Rumania abortions are only allowed if the mother's life is in danger, if she already has four children, if she is over 45 years of age, or if she is an actress or a sports star where the abortion would be in the national interest. In addition to the strict abortion law, in Rumania women are also denied the use of the birth-control pill (Alex Berg, 1972).

There is also little agreement on the abortion issue in capitalist countries. In the United States, Japan, and the Netherlands, for instance, abortion laws are as liberal as in the Soviet Union, but in West Germany a woman has no right to decide about an abortion at any time during her pregnancy. While most socialist countries guarantee their women full pay during pregnancy and a return to their jobs afterward, capitalist countries vary a great deal in the benefits they offer during and after pregnancy. South American countries offer very liberal benefits, although their marital laws are extremely restrictive for women.

It has already been pointed out that women have a double role in Russia, being frequently responsible for both factory and household work. Yorburg (1974) has pointed out that the care of infants in the family is often preferred to the day care provided by the government. It has also been discussed (see Chapter 6) that women "crowd" certain occupations in the Soviet Union as much as they do in the United States. Teaching in the lower grades is in women's hands 80 per cent of the time, and some Soviet publications express concern about "feminisazija"—about male students becoming soft and lacking initiative because they are taught by females (Butenschön, 1976).

Hilda Scott (1974) has described the status of women in Czechoslovakia; she points out that the socialist ideology to emancipate women is often abandoned in favor of material and technological requirements. Ideologically, it was the aim of Marx and Engels to free women by converting individual domestic work and child care into public industries and services. After World War II, women in Czechoslovakia were encouraged to participate in the work force and a number of programs were instituted, including child care, centralized food preparation, laundry services, and legal abortions. However, when the call for greater productivity was issued many of these services were curtailed or discontinued so that their funds and labor resources could be used more directly in production. Similarly, when the employment of women resulted in the decline in birth rate, legal abortions were restricted and ideological rationales for the importance of child-rearing and housework were offered.

From her observations on Czechoslovakia, Scott comes to the conclusion that the liberation of women will depend more on material circumstances than on ideology —regardless of the country or the social system in which it is attempted. She feels that practical programs that help women to establish economic and social independence are essential and that the maintenance of these programs would fare as well under slower and incremental reforms as under systems with more radical theories. Scott believes that women's liberation will proceed most rapidly in the more developed countries regardless of the politico-economic system because these countries will sooner reach the material basis necessary for emancipation. Scott's prediction should be modified. While a certain amount of wealth is necessary for liberation, wealth alone does not necessarily guarantee the freedom of any disadvantaged race or sex group. While the United States has the highest material wealth of any country, it is lagging behind in certain aspects of women's liberation. Other less wealthy countries offer better child-care programs, a smaller gap between the pay of males and females, pregnancy reimbursement and employment security, and more equality in their concepts of the family and of sexual activities. The government of China, for instance, puts great emphasis on the nuclear family and frowns on premarital and extramarital sex for both males and females. While this may appear restrictive to the Westerner, it may not be felt as much by the Chinese because it is a group phenomenon and avoids the double standard. While the Western countries may offer more individual alternatives to females and males, they are, in comparison to Eastern countries, far behind in closing the pay gap between the sexes.

Toward Equality

Beyond a certain level of existence, the absolute pay a person receives does not seem to be as important as the relative pay others around him or her receive. Hence in the United States and some other Western countries, an equalization in pay will be a primary condition for the equalization of the sexes. The female liberationists' demand of "equal pay for equal work" is most widely approved even by those women who are generally opposed to the liberation movement. In spite of the emphasis that this text has given to the psychological and educational aspects of sex-role equalization, it is perhaps the economic factor of equal pay through which equality could best be reached. Although dependent on attitudes and habits, the economic factor of equal pay is much more tangible and can be measured and assessed more accurately than any psychological or educational variable. As Scott suggested, once the material circumstances are altered, attitudinal changes can be expected. A mother satisfied in her employment is likely to be a model for her daughter and encourage educational motivation, etc.

Not all the economic factors are as simple to define and perhaps to control as "equal pay." "Equal work" is a much more difficult concept for which neither capitalists nor Marxists have found a convenient formula. Is the work of the secretary, who types the letters, equal to that of the manager, who dictates them? For an answer, we must ask ourselves if we mean equal in terms of importance for production, in terms of energy expanded, or in terms of preparation that the skill required. Throughout the world, the length of the training period seems to be an overriding criterion and especially if the task is mental rather than psysical. Even in many socialist countries where equal pay conditions are optimal, there are still unequal prestige factors—with the academic work being rated so high that the children of workers get preference points toward university admittance in comparison to the children of academicians in order to spread the prestige around, or at least alternate it from generation to generation. In the capitalist countries, high pay is often linked to additional conveniences and privileges where the one with higher pay has also the more comfortable job and the more flexible work schedule.

B.F. Skinner in his novel *Walden Two* (1948) describes a very fair system of work compensation. Fewer points are given for work preferred than for work not preferred. If three workers show up for a grass-mowing detail and only one for emptying the septic tank, then the latter would receive three times as much credit and would have to work only a third of the time to reach his or her quota. In reality the problem of defining "equal work" has created many difficulties among men and also among women; but it has created an especially unfair condition for women because many of the occupations in which they work are considered unequal (less important, lower in prestige, etc.) than those occupations in which males work. This inequality occurs in spite of the fact that these female and male workers may belong to the same production team—such as the female secretary and the male office manager or the female nurse and the male doctor.

The "equal work" problem should first be approached through education, and the aim should be for females to obtain scientific knowledge and skills so that they can participate in equal numbers in the technological occupations. To obtain this goal, several educational practices believed to further educational and social equality should be reexamined. As already mentioned (see Chapter 5) the elective system with regard to scientifc subjects and the required taking of linguistic subjects compensates for the boys' lack of interest in linguistic subjects but not for the girls' reluctance toward the natural sciences. Coeducation may also be hindering. At the college level, it has been found (Ormerod, 1976) that females in coeducational institutions harbor more prejudice against physics, chemistry, and mathematics than females in all-women colleges, where they do not seem to develop the notion that the natural sciences are "male" subjects.

Our concepts of equal work could also be changed by instituting a more equitable pay system within and between production teams. For example, the task of writing letters would be perceived as more equal to the task of dictating them if both activities were more equally remunerated. Economically, it would be the same whether the secretary (usually female) received $10,000 per year and the manager (usually male) $18,000 per year or whether both received $14,000.

To pay a secretary and a boss equal salary would in our present way of thinking mean "equal pay for unequal work," but the definition of "equal" as we have seen is rather arbitrary. Undoubtedly, it would require many changes in attitudes, habits, and legislation to even approach equal pay for any type of work, although it should be economically and psychologically feasible. It is interesting to note that our progressive tax structure works toward such an equilibrium, requiring those who earn more money to pay a higher percentage of taxes. Overtly, however, we are not very willing to reduce the differences between our gross incomes.

The road to equality has not been and will not be without "role-conflict" or "role-strain." Mirra Komarovsky (1946, 1973, 1974), who has analyzed role conflicts for three decades, found that they existed in the 1940s as well as in the 1970s although they have changed in intensity. In the 1940s women in Eastern colleges experienced uncertainty and insecurity because of the role conflict between academic career and housewife duties. The males also had conflicts. About 30 per cent of them felt insecure in their relationship to women. They wanted to talk to intellectual women but desired deep relationships and sex with less intellectual ones. Some males solved their dilemma by selective dating or avoidance, and some females found a solution by "playing dumb."

In the 1970s many of the conflicts of the college population have been weakened. The males seem to have reversed their notions on the female intellect with the majority now valuing competence, resourcefulness, and intelligence in their female friends. The females also experience fewer conflicts between their intellectual and psychological resources. In spite of certain mutual expectations, or perhaps on account of them, some contradictions and inconsistencies persist. Both females and males, for instance, wish careers for women, but they also have the desire that the wife accepts the full-time mother role when the children are young.

The mother-work issue has been investigated in more detail by Yorburg and Arafat (1975). Questioning more than 1,000 men and women with diverse backgrounds and professions, they found that the great majority (90 per cent of the females; 80 per cent of the males) advocated the dual role (gainful employment and homemaking) for women.

However, only about half the women and half the men approved of this dual role when children under the age of six were involved. While men and women are in essential agreement on work and household matters, they agree least on such questions as "Who should take care of infants?" "Who should straighten up the house?" and "Who should do the laundry?" They agree closest on such details as "Who should make the bed?" (perhaps neither) and "Who should go shopping?" (both).

In comparison with the past, Komarovski describes the present sex-role trend as "modified traditionalism." In terms of percentages, Yorburg and Arafat found that about 25 per cent of both sexes believe that equality of the sexes will exist someday and that about half the men and half the women believe that it will not occur. In the same vein, the majority of the sexes believe that the childhood conditioning of boys and girls into "feminine" and "masculine" roles will have to be modified somewhat to achieve greater, but not total, equality.

Although this text has dealt in some detail with the development of sex stereotypes in infancy and early childhood, a specific sex-role training for children cannot be recommended. Many of the cues by which stereotypes are established are unknown and unintentionally modeled by parents and peers. Even if a unified training approach were feasible, its final direction would still be in question as we do not know how much competition and aggression or how much patience and gentleness our economic and political future will require. Since much of the sex-role stereotypy is transmitted through modeling it would be psychologically sound if a society accomplished the desired changes first on the adult level—practicing what it preaches—so that young females have models of occupations with an equal proportion of females and males having equal status and receiving equal pay.

It would be difficult to find enough female models for those professions that require prolonged periods of training. It can be argued that the models should be there before the training begins to arouse interest and to sustain motivation. Ironically, television, which has supported the proverbial sex-role stereotypy for years, could conveniently serve to present and emphasize females in professions in which their number is rare. By selecting material from different countries, the work of females in almost every profession could be shown, including female astronauts, pilots, engineers, police personnel, physicians, and dentists.

On the individual level, parents can present their children alternatives with regard to male and female toys, games, and activities. In general, society will accept masculinity in girls more readily than femininity in boys. A girl could be given the alternative of wearing skirts or pants, but a boy is best not given this choice unless he lives in a community where he will not suffer from wearing a skirt. Children need not carry the brunt when society needs to change its norms. When given reasonable alternatives, the majority of children will engage in same-sex as well as cross-sex activities. A child who by chance or by inclination selects only one of the alternatives need not be discouraged, as the sexes can reach equality with both groups having members who are masculine, androgynous, and feminine. The broader the spectrum of our characteristics, the greater will be our chance for adaptation and survival.

Psychologists have perhaps overemphasized the concepts of femininity, masculinity, and androgyny, thereby giving the impression that these categories involve distinct and deep-rooted personality traits—traits that need to be overcome to bring about sexual equality. Radical personality changes may not be necessary, as equalization could be reached by "role-sharing." Each sex could engage in some of the activities of the other without basically changing its own characteristics. For example, a man could be dominant and aggressive and he could nevertheless do a proficient job changing diapers and doing the family wash. Neither need a woman give up her feminine characteristics (be it empathy or emotions) to change a tire proficiently. Initially it may be least conflictual for both sexes to change small units of specific behaviors than to change their basic attitudes. Komorovsky (1973) also believes that mores tend to be changed by ritual, by small variations in behavior and habit, and eventually by changes in attitudes. An emphasis on a behavioral change has the additional advantage in that it would not lend credence to those who profess equalitarian beliefs but who are traditional and stereotyped in their behavior.

REFERENCES

Acheson, R. M. Maturation of the skeleton. In F. Faulkner (Ed.) *Human Development*, Philadelphia: Saunders, 1966.

Aletky, P. J., & Carlin, A. S. Sex differences and placebo effects: Motivation as an intervening variable. *Journal of Consulting and Clinical Psychology*. 1975, *43*, 278.

Anastasi, A. *Psychological testing*. (3rd Ed.) New York: Macmillan, 1968.

Archer, J. Biology and psychological sex differences. Report: British Psychological Society, Nottingham, England, 1975.

Asher, S. R. & Gottman, J. M. Sex of teacher and student reading achievement. *Journal of Educational Psychology*, 1974, Vol. *65* (2) 168–171.

Ausubel, D. P. *Theory and problems of adolescent development*. New York: 1954.

Ballweg, J. A. Resolution of conjugal role adjustment after retirement. *Journal of Marriage and the Family*. 1967, *29*, 277–281.

Ban, P. L. & Lewis, M. Mothers and fathers, girls and boys: Attachment behavior in the one-year-old. *Merrill-Palmer Quarterly*, 1974, *20*, 195–204.

Bandura, A. Influence of models' reinforcement contingencies on the acquisition of imitative responses. *Journal of Personality and Social Psychology*, 1965, *1*, 589–595.

Bandura, A. *Principles of behavior modification.* New York: Holt, Rinehart & Winston, 1969.

Bandura, A. (Ed.) *Psychological modeling: Conflicting theories.* Chicago, Ill.: Aldine-Atherton Publ. Co., 1971.

Bandura, A. *Aggression: A social learning analysis.* Englewood Cliffs, N.J.: Prentice-Hall, 1973.

Bayley, N. Some psychological correlates of somatic androgyny. *Child Development,* 1951, *22,* 47–60.

Bayley, N. Behavioral correlates of mental growth: Birth to 36 years. *American Psychologist,* 1968, *23,* 1–17.

Bayley, N. Development of mental abilities. In P. H. Mussen (Ed.) *Carmichael's Manual of Child Psychology,* Vol. 1 (3rd Ed.).

Bayley, N., & Bayer, L. The assessment of somatic androgyny. *American Journal of Physical Anthropology,* 1946, *4,* 433–461.

Bayley, N., & Schaefer, E. S. Correlations of maternal and child behaviors with the development of mental abilities: Data from the Berkeley Growth Studies. *Monograph Society Research in Child Development,* 1964, Serial No. 97, Vol. *29,* No. 6.

Beauvoir, S. de "Das ewig Weibliche ist eine Lüge" (The eternal womanhood is a lie) *Der Spiegel,* 1976, *30,* (15) 190–201.

Beauvoir, S. de *The second sex.* New York: Knopf, 1951.

Beauvoir, S. de Interview with Betty Friedan. *Der Spiegel,* 1976.

Bell, R. Q., & Costello, N. S. Three tests for sex differences in tactile sensitivity in the newborn. *Biologia Neonatorum,* 1964, *7,* 335–347.

Bell, R. Q., & Darling, J. F. The prone head reaction in the human neonate. *Child Development,* 1965, *36,* 943–949.

Bem, S. L. The measurement of psychological androgyny. *Journal of Consulting and Clinical Psychology,* 1974, *42,* 155–162.

Bem, S. L. Sex role adoptability: One consequence of psychological androgyny. *Journal of Personality and Social Psychology,* 1975, *31,* (4) 634–643.

Bem, S. L. Die harten und die zarten. *Psychologie heute,* 1976, *3,* (2), 54–59.

Berg, A. *Sex im Sozialismus* (Sex in socialism). München: Wilhelm Heyne Verlag, 1972.

Bickman, L. Sex and helping behavior. *The Journal of Social Psychology,* 1974, *93,* 43–53.

Biller, H. & Meredith, D. *Father power.* New York: McKay Co., 1974.

Birk, J. Interest inventories: A mixed blessing. *Vocational Guidance Quarterly,* 1974, *22,* (4) 280–286.

Blackstone, T., & Fulton, O. Sex discrimination among university teachers: A British-American comparison. *The British Journal of Sociology,* 1975, XXVI, (2), 261–270.

Blake, J. The changing status of women in developed countries. *Scientific American*, 1974, (Sept.) *231*, (3) 136–147.

Book, H. M. A psychological analysis of sex differences. *Journal of Social Psychology*, 1932, *3*, 436.

Broverman, D. M., Broverman, I. K., Vogel, W., Palmer, R. D., & Glaiber, E. L. Roles of activation and inhibition in sex differences in cognitive abilities, 1968. *Psychological Review*, 1968, *75*, 23–51.

Brown, D. G. Sex-role preference in young children. *Psychological Monographs*, 1956, *70*, (14) 1–19.

Butenschön, M. Emanzipation in der UdSSR. *Die Zeit*, 1975, (Nov.) (48) p. 76.

Butenschön, M. Mangel an Männern (Shortage of men). *Frankfurter Rundschau*, 1976, April 28.

Calkins, M. W. Critical comments on the Gestalt theory. *Psychological Review*, 1926, *33*, 135–158.

Cameron, J., Livson, N. & Bayley, N. Infant vocalizations and their relationship to mature intelligence. *Science*, 1967 (July–Aug.) *157*, 331–333.

Campbell, D. Adaption to the environment by the newborn child. *The Canadian Psychologist*, 1968, *9*, 467–473.

Cattell, R. B., Blewett, D. B., & Beloff, J. R. The inheritance of personality. *American Journal of Human Genetics*, 1955, *7*, 122–146.

Cohen, D. B. Sex-role orientation and dream recall. *Journal of Abnormal Psychology*, 1973, *82*, 246–252.

Constantinople, A. Masculinity-Femininity: An exception to a famous dictum? *Psychological Bulletin*, 1973, *80* (5) 389–407.

Cramer, P., & Hogan, K. A. Sex differences in verbal and play fantasy. *Developmental Psychology*, 1975, *11*, (2), 145–154.

De Lucia, L. A. The toy-preference test: A measurement of sex-role identification. *Child Development*, 1963, *34*, 107–117.

Department of Employment *Women and work: A review*. Manpower Paper No. 11, London: Her Majesty's Stationer's Office, 1975.

Der Spiegel Neue Weiblichkeit (New Womanhood). December 1975.

Dion, K. K. Children's physical attractiveness and sex determinants of adult punitiveness. *Developmental Psychology*, 1974, *10*, 772–778.

Dion, K. K., & Berscheid, E. Physical attractiveness and peer perception among children. *Sociometry*, 1974, *34*, 1–12.

Dodge, N. T. *Women in the Soviet economy*. Baltimore: Johns Hopkins University Press, 1966.

Dwyer, C. A. Influence of children's sex role standard on reading and arithmetic achievement. *Journal of Educational Psychology*, 1974, *66*, (6) 811–816.

Eaton, G. G. The social order of Japanese macaques. *Scientific American,* 1976, October, 97–106.

Eichorn, D. Variations in growth rate. *Childhood Education,* 1968, *44,* (5), 286–291.

Ekehammar, B. Sex differences in self-reported anxiety for different stituations and modes of responses. *Scandinavian Journal of Psychology,* 1974, *15,* 154–160.

Epstein, M. L. Sex differences in incidental learning and recall of related and unrelated word pairs. *Journal of Psychology,* 1974, *88,* 3–8.

Essex, D., Parrott, G., & Barnes, P. Horizontality training at three to nine years. Paper presented at Western Psychological Association, San Francisco, April, 1971.

Etaugh, C., Collins, G., and Gerson, A. Reinforcement of sex-typed behaviors of two-year-old children in a nursery school setting. *Developmental Psychology,* 1975, *11,* 255.

Eysenck, H. J. *Manual for the Maudsley Personality Inventory.* London: University of London Press, 1959.

Eysenck, H. J. *Fact and fiction in psychology.* Baltimore: Penguin Books, 1968.

Eysenck, H. J., & Eysenck, S. B. G. *Personality structure and measurement.* London: Routlage & Kagan Paul, Ltd. 1969, 1970.

Fagot, B. I., & Patterson, G. An in vivo analysis of reinforcing contingencies for sex-role behaviors in the preschool child. *Developmental Psychology,* 1969, *1,* 563–568.

Fagot, B. I. Sex-related stereotyping of toddlers' behavior. *Developmental Psychology,* 1973, *9,* 429.

Fagot, B. I. Sex differences in toddlers' behavior and parental reaction. *Developmental Psychology,* 1974, *10,* 554–558.

Feather, N. T., and Raphelson, A. C. Fear of success in Australian and American student groups: Motive or sex-role stereotype? *Journal of Personality,* 1974, *42,* (2) 190–201.

Fein, G., Johnson, D., Kosson, N., Stork, L., & Wasserman, L. Sex stereotypes and preferences in toy choices of 20-month-old boys and girls. *Developmental Psychology,* 1975, *11,* 527–528.

Fisher, S. *Body experience in fantasy and behavior.* New York: Appleton-Century-Crofts, 1970.

Fisher, S. *The female orgasm: Psychology, physiology, fantasy.* New York: Basic Books, 1973.

Fling, S., & Manosevith, M. Sex-typing in nursery school children's play interests. *Developmental Psychology,* 1972, *7,* (2), 146–152.

Focke, K. In Grosse erotische Mutter (Big erotic mother). *Der Spiegel,* 1975, *29,* (27) 31–41.

Franks, A. & Berg, K. W. Effects of visual complexity and sex of infant in the conjugate reinforcement paradigm. *Developmental Psychology,* 1975, *11*, (3), 388–389.

Freeman, J. The origins of the women's liberation movement. *American Journal of Sociology,* 1973, *78*, (4), 792–811.

Freud, Sigmund *Abriss der Psychoanalyse* (Outline of psychoanalysis) 1939 (published posthumously) New York: Norton, 1940.

Freud, Sigmund *Gesammelte Werke.* (Collected papers) 1892–1939. Vol. 1–17, Frankfurt: Fisher Verlag, 1968.

Friedan, B. *The feminine mystique.* New York: Dell, 1963.

Friedan, B. In Grosse erotische Mutter (Big erotic mother). *Der Spiegel,* 1975, *29*, (27) 31–41.

Fryrear, J. L., & Thelen, M. H. The effect of sex of model and sex of observer on the imitation of affectionate behavior. *Developmental Psychology,* 1969, *1*, 298.

Fuchs, V. R. Differences in hourly earnings between men and women. *Monthly Labor Review,* 1971, *94*, 9–15.

Fuchs, V. R. A note on sex segregation in professional occupations. *Explorations in Economics Research,* 1975, *2*, 105–111.

Gall, M. D. The relationship between masculinity-femininity and manifest anxiety. *Journal of Clinical Psychology,* 1969, *25*, 294–295.

Gardiner, C. H. Chess survey. Unpublished report. Portland State University, 1974.

Gaspeed, L., Peterson, J. A., Stockwell, L., Sause, C., & Templeman, B. An investigation of sexism in songs used in the primary grades. Workshop project, Portland State University, Summer 1973.

Gilbert, S. D. *What's a father for?* New York: Parents' Magazine Press, 1975.

Ginzberg, E. *Life styles of educated women.* New York: Columbia University Press, 1966.

Glass, S. J. & Johnson, R. W. Limitations and complications of organotherapy in male homosexuality. *Journal of Clinical Endocrinology,* 1944, *4*, 540.

Goldberg, M. S. Can the faltering feminist movement regain its old momentum and magic? *Saturday Review,* June 14, 1975, 22–24.

Goldberg, S., & Lewis, M. Play behavior in the year-old infant: Early sex differences. *Child Development,* 1969, *40*, 21–31.

Good, T. L., Sikes, J. N., & Brophy, J. E. Effects of teacher sex and student sex on classroom interaction. *Journal of Educational Psychology,* 1973, *65*, (1), 74–87.

Gough, H. G. Identifying psychological femininity, *Educational and Psychological Measurement,* 1952, *12*, 427–439.

Gough, H. G., & Heilbrun, A. B. *Adjective check list manual.* Palo Alto, Calif.: Consulting Psychologists Press, 1965.

Govatos, L. A. Relationships and age differences in growth measures and motor skills. *Child Development,* 1959, *30,* 333–340.

Gove, W., & Tudor, J. Adult sex roles and mental illness. *American Journal of Sociology,* 1973, *78,* 812–835.

Gubbels, R. The supply and demand for women workers. Regional Trade Union Seminar, Paris, 1970. Also in N. Glazer-Malbin and H. Youngelson-Waehrer (Eds.) *Woman in a man-made world.* Chicago: Rand McNally, 1972.

Guilford, J. P., & Guilford, R. B. Personality factors S, E, and M and their measurement. *Journal of Psychology,* 1936 2, 109–127.

Gutteridge, M. V. A study of motor achievements of young children. *Arch. Psych. N. Y.,* 1939, No. 244.

Hall, D. T. and Gordon, F. Career choices of married women: Effects on conflict, role behavior, and satisfaction. *Journal of Applied Psychology.* 1973, Vol. 58 (1) 42–48.

Hamburg, D. A. Recent research on hormonal factors relevant to human aggressiveness. *International Social Science Journal,* 23 (1) Paris, UNESCO, 1971, 36–47. Also in: *Woman in a man-made world.* N. Glazer-Malbin & H. Youngelson-Waehrer (Eds.) Rand McNally, 1972.

Hamner, W. C., Kim, J. S., Baird, L., & Bigoness W. J. Race and sex as determinants of rating by potential employers in a simulated work-sample task. *Journal of Applied Psychology.* 1974, 59 (6) 705–711.

Handbook on women workers. Washington, D.C.: United States Government Printing Office, 1969.

Harford, T. C., Willis, C. H., & Deabler, H. L. Personality correlates of masculinity-femininity. *Psychological Reports,* 1967, *21,* 881–884.

Harlow, H. F. Love in infant monkeys. *Scientific American* 200, (6), 1959, 68–74.

Harris, L. Opinion Poll, Princeton, N.J., 1971.

Hartley, R. Sex-role pressures and the socialization of the male child. *Psychological Reports,* 1967, *20,* 457–468.

Hartley, R., Hardesty, F. P., & Gorfein, D. S. Children's perception and expressions of sex preferences. *Child Development,* 1962, *33,* 221–227.

Hartnett, O. Sex role steryotyping and occupational psychology. Paper presented at the meeting of the British Psychological Society. Nottingham, April 1975.

Havelick, R., & Vane, J. Race, competency, and level of achievement: Relationship to modeling in elementary school children. *The Journal of Psychology,* 1974, (May) 53–57.

Heinstein, M. I. Behavioral correlates of breast-bottle regimes under varying parent-infant relationships. *Monographs of the Society for Research in Child Development,* 28, (4) Ser: 88. 1963.

Held, T., & Levy, R., *Die Stellung der Frau in Familie und Gesellschaft* (Position of the woman in family and society). Stuttgart: Verlag Huber, 1974.

Herrnstein, R. J. *Chancengleichheit eine Utopie?* Stuttgart: Deutsche Verlags Anstalt, 1974.

Hochschild, A. R. A review of sex-role research. *American Journal of Sociology,* 1973, *78,* (4) 1011–1029.

Hoffman, H. N., & Maier, N. R. F. Sex differences, sex composition and group problem solving. *Journal of Abnormal and Social Psychology,* 1961, *63,* 453–456.

Hoffman, L. W. Fear of success in males and females: 1965–1971. *Journal of Consulting and Clinical Psychology.* 1974, *42,* (3) 353–358.

Honzik, M. Environmental correlates of mental growth: Prediction from the family setting at 12 months. *Child Development,* 1967, *38,* 337–364.

Horner, M. S. Sex differences in achievement motivation and performance in competitive and non-competitive situations. Unpublished doctoral dissertation, University of Michigan, 1968.

Hottes, J., & Kahn, A. Sex differences in a mixed-motive conflict situation. *Journal of Personality,* 1974, *42,* 260–273.

Hutt, C. *Males and females.* Harmondsworth, England: Penguin Books, 1972.

Jackson, R. L. & Kelly, M. G. Growth charts for use in pediatrics practice. *Journal of Pediatrics,* 1945, *27,* 213–229.

Jenkins, L. M. *Comparative study of motor achievements of children 5, 6, & 7 years of age.* New York: Teachers College Press, Columbia University, 1930.

Jensen, A. R. How much can we boost I.Q. and scholastic achievement? *Harvard Educational Review,* 1969, *39,* 1–123.

Jones, M. C. The elimination of children's fears. *Journal of Experimental Psychology,* 1924, *7,* 382–390.

Karmel, L. J. *Measurement and evaluation in the schools.* New York: Macmillan, 1970.

Kinsey, A. C., Pomeroy, W., Martin, C., & Gebhard, P. *Sexual behavior in the human female.* Philadelphia: Saunders, 1953.

Kohlberg, L. A. Cognitive-developmental analysis of children's sex-role concepts and attitudes. In E. Maccobu (Ed.) *The development of sex differences.* Palo Alto, Calif.: Stanford University Press, 1966.

Komarovsky, M. Cultural contradiction and sex roles. *American Journal of Sociology,* 1946, *51,* 182–189.

Komarovsky, M. Cultural contradictions and sex roles: The masculine case. *American Journal of Sociology,* 1973, *78,* (4), 873–884.

Komarovsky, M. Some problems in role analysis. *American Sociological Review,* 1974, *38,* (6), 649–662.

Korner, A. F. Neonatal startles, smiles, erections and reflex sucks as related to state, sex, and individuality. *Child Development,* 1969, *40,* 1039–1053.

Kostich, M. M. Study of transfer: Sex differences in the reasoning process. *Journal of Educational Psychology,* 1954, *45,* 449–458.

Kroger, W. S., & Freed, S. C. Psychosomatic aspects of frigidity. *Journal American Medical Association.* 1950, *143,* 526–532.

Kuder, G. F. *Kuder preference record-vocational manual and Kuder preference record personal: manual.* Chicago: Science Research Associates, 1948, 1953.

Kunstmann, A. *Frauenemanzipation und Erziehung* (Women emancipation and education) 3rd Ed. Starnberg, Germany: Werner Raith Verlag, 1973.

Ladd-Franklin, C. *Colour and colour theories.* New York: Harcourt Brace, 1929.

Lehman, H. C., & Witty, P. A. *The psychology of play activities.* New York: Barnes, 1927.

Lehr, U. Das Problem der Sozialization geschlechts-spezifischer Verhaltensweisen. (The problem of the socialization of sex-role behavior). *Handbuch der Psychology,* Vol. II, No. 7, Göttingen, Verlag Hogrefe, 1972.

Levin, R., & Levin, A. Sexual pleasures: The surprising preferences of 100,000 women. *Redbook,* September 1975, 51–58.

Lipman-Blumen, J. How ideology shapes women's lives. *Scientific American,* 1972, *222,* (1), 34–42.

Lipsitt, L. P., & Levy, N. Pain threshold in the human neonate. *Child Development,* 1959, *30,* 547–554.

Lipsitt, L. P., Weisberg, P., & Kaye, H. *Learning in infants.* Motion picture (30 min., 16 mm.) Blender Films, 1967.

Lomranz, J., Shapira, A., Choresh, N., & Gilat, Y. Children's personal space as a function of age and sex. *Developmental Psychology,* 1975, *11,* 541–545.

Looft, W. Sex differences in the expression of vocational aspirations by elementary school children. *Developmental Psychology,* 1971, *5,* 366.

Lyle, J., & Ross, J. L. *Women in industry.* Lexington, Ma.: Lexington Books, 1973.

Lynn, D. B. *Parental and sex role identification.* Berkeley, Calif.: McCuthan Publishing Corp., 1969.

Maccoby, E. E., & Jacklin, C. N. Sex differences and their implication for sex roles. Paper: American Psychological Association, Washington, D.C. Sept. 1971.

Maccoby, E. E., & Jacklin, C. N. *The psychology of sex differences.* Palo Alto, Calif.: Stanford University Press, 1974.

Machover, K. *Personality projection in the drawings of the human figure.* Springfield, Ill.: Charles Thomas, 1949.

Madden, J. F. *The economics of sex discrimination.* Lexington, Ma.: Lexington Books, 1973.

Madigan, F. C. Are sex mortality differentials biologically caused? *Millbank Memorial Fund Quarterly,* 1957, (April) *35,* (2) 202–223.

Margolin, G. & Patterson, G. Differential consequences provided by mothers and fathers for their sons and daughters. *Developmental Psychology,* 1975, *11,* 537–538.

Marquis, D. Can conditioned responses be established in the newborn infant? *Journal of Genetic Psychology,* 1931, *39,* 479–492. Also in: P. H. Mussen, J. J. Conger, & J. Kagan (Eds.) *Readings in child psychology and personality.* New York: Harper & Row, 1965.

Masters, W. H., & Johnson, V. E. *Human sexual response.* Boston: Little Brown, 1966.

Masters, W. H., & Johnson, V. E. *Human sexual inadequacy.* Boston: Little Brown, 1970.

Matussek, P. Funktionelle Sexualstörungen (Functional sexual disturbances) In Hans Giese (Ed.) *Die Sexualität des Menschen* (Human Sexuality) Stuttgart: Ferdinand Enke Verlag, 1971.

May, R. B., & Hutt, C. Modality and sex differences in recall and recognition memory. *Child Development,* 1974, *45,* 228–231.

McCall, R. B. Exploration manipulation and play in the human infant. *Monographs of the Society for Research in Child Development,* 1974, *39,* (2).

McCall, R. B., & Kagan, J. Attention in the infant: effects of complexity, contour, perimeter and familiarity. *Child Development,* 1967, *38,* 939–952.

McCall's Magazine "Right Now," April 1976, 87–94.

McCandless, B. R., & Evans, E. D. *Children and youth: Psychological development.* Hinsdale, Il.: Dryden Press, 1973.

McEwen, B. S. Interaction between hormones and nerve tissue *Scientific American,* 1976, *235,* (1) July, 48–58.

McGinnies, E., Nordholm, L. A., Ward C. D., & Bhanthumnavin, D. Z. Sex and cultural difference in perceived locus of control among students in five countries. *Journal of Consulting and Clinical Psychology,* 1974, *42,* 541–555.

Mead, M. *Sex and temperament in three primitive societies.* New York: Morrow, 1935.

Messer, S. B., & Lewis, M. Social class and sex differences in the attachment and play behavior of the one-year-old infant, *Merrill Palmer Quarterly,* 1972, *18,* 295–306.

Millett, K. *Sexual politics.* Garden City, N.Y.: Doubleday, 1971.

Mischel, H. N. Sex bias in the evaluation of professional achievements. *Journal of Educational Psychology,* 1974, *66,* 157–166.

M M P I Handbook Vol. 1, (Rev. Ed.) Minneapolis: University of Minnesota Press, 1972.

Money, J., & Ehrhardt, A. A. *Man and woman, boy or girl.* Baltimore: Johns Hopkins University Press, 1972.

Montemayor, R. Children's performance in a game and their attraction to it as a function of sex-typed labels. *Child Development,* 1974, *45,* 152–156.

Moore, T. Language and intelligence: A longitudinal study of the first eight years. *Human Development,* 1967, *10,* 88–106.

Moran, R. D. Reducing discrimination: Role of the Equal Pay Act. *Monthly Labor Review,* 1970 (June) 30–34.

Moss, H. A. Sex, age, and state as determinants of mother-infant interaction. *Merrill-Palmer Quarterly,* 1967, *13,* 19–36.

Munsinger, H. Most California college women already know that the surface of still water is always horizontal. *The American Journal of Psychology,* 1974, *87,* 717–718.

Murdock, G. P. *Social structures.* New York: Macmillan, 1949.

Mussen, P. Some antecedents and consequences of masculine sex-typing in adolescent boys. *Psychological Monographs,* 1961, *75,* No. 506, 1–24.

Mussen, P. Long-term consequents of masculinity of interest in adolescence. *Journal of Consulting Psychology,* 1962, *26,* 435–440.

Nash, J. *Developmental psychology: A psychobiological approach.* Englewood Cliffs, N. J.: Prentice-Hall, 1970.

Nave-Herz, R. Die Ziele der Frauenbewegung: Eine Inhaltsanalyse der Emanzipations-Literatur von 1968–1973. (The aims of the women's movement: Content analysis of the emancipation literature from 1968 to 1973). In: *Politik und Zeitgeschichte,* Bonn: 1975.

Nichols, J. *Men's liberation: A new definition of masculinity.* New York: Penguin Books, 1975.

Ormerod, M. Brunel University Report. *Hamburger Abendblatt,* May 15/16, 1976.

Pendergrass, V. E., Kimmel, E., Joesting, J., Peterson, J., & Bush, E. Sex discrimination counseling. *American Psychologist,* 1976 (Jan), 36–46.

Peterson, C. C., & Peterson, J. L. Preference for sex of offspring as a measure of change in sex attitudes. *Psychology*, 1973, *10*, 3–5.

Piaget, J., & Inhelder, B. *The child's conception of space.* New York: Norton, 1967.

Piddington, R. *An introduction to social anthropology.* (Vol. I). Edinburgh: Oliver & Boyd, 1957.

Pietrofesa, J., & Schlossberg, N. Counselor bias and the female occupational role. In N. Glazer-Malbin and H. Youngelson-Waehrer (Eds.) *Woman in a man-made world.* Chicago: Rand McNally, 1972.

Pleck, J. H. Masculinity-Femininty: Current and alternate paradigms. *Sex Roles*, 1975, *1* (2) 161–178.

Portuges, S. H., & Feshbach, N. D. The influence of sex and socioethnic factors upon imitation of teachers by elementary schoolchildren. *Child Development*, 1972, *43*, 981–989.

Price, E. Chess Survey, Unpublished report, Portland State University, 1974.

Pross, H. in *Der Spiegel*, 1975, *29*, (27), 31–41.

Radloff, L. Sex differences in depression: The effects of occupation and marital status. *Sex Roles*, 1975, *1*, (3) 249–265.

Rainer, J. D. The contributions of Franz Josef Kallmann to the genetics of schizophrenia. *Behavioral Science*, 1955, *11*, 413–437.

Rasche, C. in *Seattle Times*, April 1976.

Rebelsky, F., & Hanks, C. Fathers' verbal interaction with infants in the first three months of life. *Child Development*, 1971, *42*, 63–68.

Rees, A. H., & Palmer, F. H. Factors related to change in mental test performance. *Developmental Psychology Monographs*, 1970, *3*, (2) Part 2, 1–57.

Reppucci, N. D. Parental education, sex differences, and performance on cognitive tasks among two-year-old children. *Developmental Psychology*, 1971, *4*, 248–253.

Rosen, B., & Jerdee, T. H. Effects of applicant's sex and difficulty of job on evaluations of candidates for managerial positions. *Journals of Applied Psychology.* 1974 a, *59* (4) 511–512.

Rosen, B., & Jerdee, T. H. Influence of sex-role stereotypes on personal decisions. *Journal of Applied Psychology.* 1974 b, *59*, (1) 9–14.

Rosenberg, B. G., & Sutton-Smith, B. A revised conception of masculine-feminine differences in play activities. *The Journal of Genetic Psychology*, 1960, *96*, 165–170.

Rosenkrantz, P., Vogel, S., Bee, H., Boverman, I., & Boverman, D. M. Sex-role stereotypes and self-conception of college students. *Journal of Consulting and Clinical Psychology*, 1968, *32*, 287–295.

Rubin, J. Z., Provenzano, F. J., & Luria, Z. The eye of the beholder: Parents' view on sex of newborns. *American Journal of Orthopsychiatry,* 1974, *44,* 512–519.

Samuels, J., & Turnure, J. E. Attention and reading achievement in first-grade boys and girls. *Journal of Educational Psychology,* 1974, *66,* (1) 29–32.

Sauls, J. M., & Larson, R. C. Exploring national assessment data using singular value decomposition. Education Commission of the States, Denver, April 1975.

Schaefer, L. C. Sexual experiences and reactions of a group of 30 women as told to a female psychologist. Unpublished doctoral dissertation. Columbia University, 1964.

Schaffer, H. R., & Emerson, P. E. Patterns of response to physical contact in early human development. *Journal of Child Psychology and Psychiatry,* 1964, *5,* 1–13.

Schlaegel, J., Schoof-Tams, K., & Walczak, L. Sexuelle Sozialisation in Vorpubertät, Pubertät und früher Adoleszens. (Sexual socialization: Pre-puberty, puberty, and early adolescence). I–II. *Sexualmedizin,* 1975, *4,* (4–6).

Schmidt, H. D. Einstellung und offenes Verhalten (Attitudes and overt behavior). *Psychologie Heute,* 1976. *3* (2) Feb. 29–33.

Schofield, M. *The sexual behavior of young people.* London: Longmans Green, 1965.

Scott, H. *Does socialism liberate women?* Boston: Beacon Press, 1974.

Scrimshaw, N. S., & Young, V. R. The requirements of human nutrition. *Scientific American,* 1976, Vol 255 (3) Sept. 51–64.

Sears, R. R. Relation of early socialization experiences to self concepts and gender role in middle childhood. *Child Development,* 1970, *41,* 267–289.

Selg, H. *Menschliche Aggressivitat,* Gottingen, Germany: Verlag Hogrefe, 1974.

Shephard, W. O., & Hess, D. T. Attitudes in four age groups toward sex role division in adult occupations and activities. *Journal of Vocational Behavior,* 1975, *6,* 27–39.

Sherfey, M. J. The evolution and nature of female sexuality in relation to psychoanalytic theory. *Journal of the American Psychoanalytic Association,* 1966, *14,* 28–128.

Shock, N. W. Physiological changes in adolescence. In: *The course of human development.* Xerox College Publications, 1971.

Sigusch, Volkmar Sexuelle Reaktionen bei der Frau (Female sexual reactions) In Hans Giese (Ed.) *Die Sexualität des Menschen* (Human sexuality) Stuttart: Enke, 1971.

Simitis, S., & Zenz, G. (Eds.) *Seminar: Familie und Familienrecht* (Family and family rights). Frankfurt: Verlag Suhrkamp, 1975.

Skinner, B. F. *Walden two.* New York: Macmillan, 1948.

Skinner, B. F. *Beyond freedom and dignity.* New York: 1971. Also: *Jenseits von Freiheit und Würde.* Hamburg: Rowohlt Verlag, 1973.

Skinner, B. F. *Contingencies of reinforcement.* New York: Appleton-Century-Crofts, 1969. Also in: *Die Funktion der Verstärkung in der Verhaltenswissenschaft.* München: Kindler Verlag, 1974.

Smith, P. C., Kendall, L. M., & Hulin, C. L. *The measurement of satisfaction in work and retirement.* Chicago: Rand McNally, 1969.

Snow, E. *Red China today.* New York: Random House, 1971.

Sorrentino, R. M., & Short, J. Effects of fear of success on women's performance at masculine versus feminine tasks. *Journal of Research in Personality.* 1974, 8, (3) 277–290.

South, E. B. Some psychological aspects of committee work. *Journal of Applied Psychology,* 1927, *11,* 348–368, & 437–464.

Spence, J. T., Helmreich, R., & Stapp, P. The personal attributes questionnaire: A measure of sex-role stereotypes and masculinity-femininity. *Catalog of Selected Documents in Psychology,* 1974, *4,* 43–44.

Spreitzer, E., Snyder, E. E., & Larson, D. Age, marital status, and labor force participation as related to life satisfaction. *Sex Roles,* 1975, *1,* (3) 235–247.

Stamps, L. E., & Porges, S. W. Heart rate conditioning in newborn infants: Relationship among conditionability, heart rate variability, and sex. *Developmental Psychology,* 1975, *11,* (4), 424–431.

Statistisches Jahrbuch 1975 (Statistical Yearbook, 1975). Germany: Verlag Kohlhammer, 1975.

Steinhausen, H. C. Zur Psychologie der chronischen Krankheit: Untersuchungen an Hemophilen. (The psychology of chronic diseases: Investigating hemophiliacs) Dissertation, University of Hamburg, Germany, 1976.

Stephan, C. Sex prejudice in jury simulation. *The Journal of Psychology,* 1974, *88,* 305–312

Sternglanz, S., & Serbin, L. A. Sex role stereotyping in children's television programs. *Developmental Psychology,* 1974, *10,* 710–715.

Stinnett, N., Farris, J. A., & Walters, J. Parent-child relationships of male and female high school students. *The Journal of Genetic Psychology,* 1974, *125,* 99–106.

Stolz, R. H., & Stolz, L. M. *Somatic development of adolescent boys: A study of the growth of boys during the second decade of life,* New York: Macmillan, 1951.

Strong, E. K. *Vocational interest blank for women: Manual for men: Manual.* Palo Alto, Calif.: Stanford University Press, 1951.

Suchner, R. W., & More, D. M. Stereotypes of males and females in two occupations. *Journal of Vocational Behavior.* 1975, *6,* 1–8.

Sutton-Smith, B. *Child psychology.* New York: Appleton-Century-Crofts, 1973.

Sutton-Smith, B., & Sovasta, M. Sex differences in play and power. Paper: Eastern Psychological Association, Boston, April 1972.

Swensen, C., Jr. Empirical evaluations of human figure drawings. *Psychological Bulletin,* 1957, *54,* 431–466.

Tanner, J. M. *Growth at adolescence* (2nd ed.) Oxford, England: Blackwell Publishers, 1962.

Terman, L. *Genetic studies of genius,* Vol. I. Palo Alto, Calif.: Stanford University Press, 1926,

Terman, L. M., & Miles, C. *Sex and personality: Studies in masculinity and femininity.* New York: McGraw Hill, 1936.

Terman, L. M., & Merrill, M. A. *Revised Stanford-Binet Intelligence scale* (3rd Ed.) Boston: Houghton Mifflin, 1960.

Terman, L. M., & Oden, H. M. *The gifted group at mid-life: Thirty-five years of follow-up of the superior child.* Palo Alto, Calif.: Stanford University Press, 1959.

Thomas, H. The effects of social position, race, and sex on work values of ninth-grade students. *Journal of Vocational Behavior,* 1974, *4,* 357–368.

Thomas, H., Jamison, W., & Hummel, D. Observation is insufficient for discovering that the surface of still water is invariantly horizontal. *Science,* 1973, (July) Vol. 181, 173–174.

Thompson, N. L., & McCandless, B. R. It score variables by instructional style. *Child Development,* 1970, *41,* 425–436.

Time magazine, The emerging European woman. 1974, October 28, 14–21.

Time magazine, The parent gap. 1975, September 22, 48–56.

Time magazine, Womanswar. 1975, December 1, p. 55.

Time magazine, Women truckers. 1976, April 26, p. 40.

Torrance, E. P. *Guiding creative talent.* Englewood Cliffs, N. J.: Prentice-Hall, 1962.

Tresemer, D. Fear of success: Popular but unproven. *Psychology Today,* 1974, (1) 82–85.

Tyler, L. The psychology of human differences. (3rd Ed.) New York: Appleton-Century-Crofts, 1965.

U. S. News & World Report, The American Woman, December 8. 1975, 54–64.

Van Dusen, R. A., & Sheldon, E. B. The changing status of American women: A life cycle perspective. *American Psychologist,* 1976, February, 106–116.

Walberg, H. I. Physics, femininity, and creativity. *Developmental Psychology,* 1969, *1,* 47–54.

Watson, J. B., & Morgan, J. J. B. Emotional reactions and psychological experimentation. *American Journal of Psychology,* 1917, *28,* 163–174.

Watson, J. B., & Rayner, R. Conditioned emotional reactions *Journal of Experimental Psychology,* 1920, *3,* 1–14.

Watson, J. S. Operant conditioning of visual fixation in infants under visual and auditory reinforcement. *Developmental Psychology,* 1969, *1,* (5) 508–516.

Wechsler, D. Wechsler intelligence scale for children. New York: The Psychological Corporation, 1952.

Weitzman, L. J., Eifler, D., Hakoda, E., & Ross, C. Sex role socialization in children's picture books. Paper presented at the annual meeting of the Georgia Sociological and Anthropological Association, Athens, Ga., 1971. In *Sociological Abstracts,* Vol XIX, No. 7, Supplement 20.

Wesley, F. *Childrearing psychology,* New York: Behavioral Publications, 1971.

Wiechel, L. Konsrollsperception och samverkansberedskap (Sex-role attitude and co-operation readiness). Malmo, Pedagogisk Psykilogiska Institutet, 1972.

Will, J. A., Self, P. A., & Datan, N. Maternal behavior and perceived sex of infant. *American Journal of Orthopsychiatry,* 1976, *46,* (1), 135–139.

Williams, J. E., & Bennett, S. The definition of sex stereotypes via the Adjective Check List. *Sex Roles,* 1975, *1,* (4), 327–337.

Witkin, H. A., Lewis, H. B., Hirtman, M., Machover, K., Meissner, P. B. & Wapner, S. *Personality through perception,* New York: Harper, 1954.

Witkin, H. A., Dyke, R. B., Faterson, H., Goodenough, D. R., & Karp, S. A. *Psychological differentiation: Studies of development.* New York: Wiley, 1962.

Wittig, M. A. Sex differences in intellectual functioning: How much of a difference do genes make? *Sex Roles,* 1976, Vol 2 (1), 63–74.

Wolf, T. M. Effects of live modeled sex-inappropriate play behavior in a naturalistic setting. *Developmental Psychology,* 1973, *9,* 120–123.

Wolf, T. M. Influence of age and sex of model on sex-inappropriate play. *Psychological Reports,* 1975, *36* 99–105.

Woolf, V. *Orlando.* New York: Harcourt Brace, 1928.

Yorburg, B. *Sexual identity: Sex roles and social change.* New York: Wiley, 1974.

Yorburg, B., & Arafat, I. Current sex role conceptions and conflict. *Sex Roles*, 1975, *1*, (2) 135–146.

Zelig, R. Children's attitudes toward annoyance. *The Journal of Genetic Psychology*, 1962, *101*, 255–266.

SUBJECT INDEX

AUTHOR INDEX